# MATCHMAKER
# MATCHMAKER

Aleeza Ben Shalom

# MATCHMAKER
# MATCHMAKER

### Find Me
### a Love
### That Lasts

**UNION
SQUARE
& CO.**

NEW YORK

UNION
SQUARE
&CO.
NEW YORK

UNION SQUARE & CO. and the distinctive Union Square & Co.
logo are trademarks of Sterling Publishing Co., Inc.

Union Square & Co., LLC, is a subsidiary of Sterling Publishing Co., Inc.

Text © 2024 Marriage Minded Mentor, LLC

ISBN 978-1-4549-5614-3
ISBN 978-1-4549-5615-0 (e-book)

Library of Congress Cataloging-in-Publication Data

Names: Ben Shalom, Aleeza, author.
Title: Matchmaker matchmaker : find me a love that lasts / Aleeza Ben
Shalom.
Description: New York : Union Square & Co., [2024] | Includes
bibliographical references. | Summary: "In her paradigm-shifting book,
Aleeza Ben Shalom, dating coach and Netflix star, will guide readers
through her highly original perspective on dating, revealing the
surprising ways in which a person's dating habits directly influence
their chances of finding lasting love"-- Provided by publisher.
Identifiers: LCCN 2024022270 (print) | LCCN 2024022271 (ebook) | ISBN
9781454956143 (hardcover) | ISBN 9781454956150 (ebook)
Subjects: LCSH: Dating (Social customs) | Interpersonal attraction. | Mate
selection.
Classification: LCC HQ801 .B3947 2024 (print) | LCC HQ801 (ebook) | DDC
646.7/7--dc23/eng/20240702
LC record available at https://lccn.loc.gov/2024022270
LC ebook record available at https://lccn.loc.gov/2024022271

For information about custom editions, special sales, and premium purchases,
please contact specialsales@unionsquareandco.com.

Printed in Canada

2 4 6 8 10 9 7 5 3 1

unionsquareandco.com

Cover design by Erik Jacobsen
Cover photograph © 2024 Jamie Gordon
Interior design by Christine Heun

To my Mom, who taught me
everything I know
about unconditional love.

# Contents

# Introduction

Chances are you've picked up this book because you're searching for someone to spend the rest of your life with—but something isn't quite clicking. You thought true love was supposed to happen naturally, so why hasn't your partner shown up yet? Maybe you're on the apps, but finding that things fizzle after a couple of dates. Maybe you're too overwhelmed to even start putting yourself out there. Maybe no one seems to meet your criteria. Maybe you're starting to suspect self-sabotage.

If any of this rings a bell, you've probably been stuck in this pattern for long enough that either you're starting to lose hope or you feel like you're going crazy. Why is this so hard?!

I need you to take a deep breath. Let it out. Repeat.

It doesn't have to be this hard.

Don't get me wrong: it will require effort on your part. But let's make sure that effort steers you in the right direction, away from the endless cycle. That's where I come in. I'm Aleeza Ben Shalom. You might know me from Netflix's *Jewish Matchmaking*, but rest assured—the insights in this book apply to everyone, regardless of your background or religion.

This book isn't just a roadmap to finding "The One"; it's about self-discovery, understanding what truly matters in a match, and learning how to cultivate a relationship that stands the test of time.

Together, we're going to:

- ◆ Cut through distraction and overthinking.
- ◆ Step out of fantasyland and kick destructive habits to the curb.
- ◆ Help you get clear on what you want in a partner.
- ◆ Teach you to recognize those qualities when they're right in front of you.

All you have to do is keep an open mind, put effort into the connections you're making, and let time do its work. No matter what your dating challenges are (and trust me, we're going to dive into all of it), this approach will teach you plenty about the people you date, and even more about yourself. The journey to lasting love is less about finding the perfect person, and more about creating the perfect partnership. And it begins now.

Onward.

CHAPTER ONE

# Date 'Em 'Til You Hate 'Em

Dana is a child of the '90s. She came of age wearing biker shorts, swapping slap bracelets, and watching *Full House*. She was a born romantic, thanks in part to the Disney movies that taught her everything she knew about love. Her personal favorite was *The Little Mermaid*, which she watched every day after school. There was something about seeing Ariel risk it all (voice and legs included) to win the dashing Prince Eric that made Dana's heart flutter. In her mind, it was the perfect romance: Mermaid sees gorgeous prince and falls instantly in love. Mermaid saves Eric from drowning, then sings to his unconscious body. Eric awakens to see Mermaid and falls in love right back. Despite King Triton's disapproval and Ursula's scheming, Ariel triumphs, becomes permanently human, and gets her man. True love conquers all! The fact that the couple did not actually exchange a word until the end of the story was of no concern to Dana; it was clear to her that once you found your person, all the pesky details would work themselves out.

"When you know, you know," she'd say, dreaming of a prince of her own.

Fast-forward twenty-five years to find Dana in my office. Now she's thirty-two and a hotshot lawyer living on the Upper West Side. She's independent, intelligent, beautiful—a real catch. But she's still waiting for her prince to show up.

"I need my husband to be successful in his own right, or else he'll resent me," she says.

"Has that been the case with your other relationships?" I ask. Understanding my clients' dating history is essential in my line of work. "Your partners were less successful?"

"Actually, my last two were *more* successful than me, but still ended up resenting my long hours . . ." She sighs. "If I have any hope of finding my person, he needs to be able to relate to my work schedule. Although maybe not even then. Sometimes I feel like I'll have to choose: keep my career, or fall in love."

"You don't think it's possible to have both?"

"I think . . . for love, maybe you have to sacrifice everything."

Like Ariel, Dana sees two worlds that exist in opposition to each other. It's work versus love, and she can only choose one.

It's no wonder she can't find a partner: she's looking for a specific set of circumstances rather than a person. Under the assumption that only high-powered, ambitious, and successful men will understand her, Dana rules out literally thousands of candidates who might be a better match. The "happily ever after" she thinks she's supposed to choose looks nothing like the one she actually wants. So she ends up with neither.

The reason Dana can't make a relationship last is that she doesn't know how to have one in the first place.

She isn't to blame for this. Dana, like most of society, has internalized the idea that finding love is an almost magical event that's orchestrated by forces beyond your control. "Someday your prince will come"—and you'll know it's him because he'll check every box on your list. The connection is instantaneous, as is the knowledge that this is your one-and-forever person. With no effort (and, in some cases, no conversation!), all falls into place. While it's true that, as a society, we are coming around to the idea that *maintaining* a relationship requires hard work on our part, we still hold on to the notion that meeting someone should be effortless, kismet, and without any hitches.

I call this "Disney dating."

I get the appeal. I really do. Who doesn't want a simple, picture-perfect origin love story? Even *I* can't resist that moment when Aladdin melts at the first sight of Jasmine in the marketplace. But from my experience—and I've seen this happen *hundreds* of times—if you date like a two-dimensional character, you're going to have a two-dimensional relationship. In a three-dimensional world, it's no wonder that millions of Disney daters find themselves unfulfilled, frustrated, and ultimately, alone.

If Dana wants to find *real* love, she has to kick Disney dating to the curb.

Her first assignment: revise her definition of "When you know, you know."

Thus far, "When you know, you know" has been her romantic barometer—and it hasn't served her well. Why?

Because it's a cop-out.

"When you know, you know" is another way of saying, "My only job is to recognize my person when they magically show up." This philosophy absolves people of responsibility, excuses them from effort, and tricks them into mistaking physical attraction for love.

This is as far as Dana (and most people) have ever gotten.

Imagine that you wanted a promotion at work. Would you sit and wait for your boss to hand it to you? No way! You'd show up early, leave late, take on extra projects, and beat all your deadlines. You wouldn't rest until that promotion was yours.

In other words, you'd work for it.

Why shouldn't the same go for finding your person?

Love is not always something that just happens; it can be cultivated intentionally, like a good habit. This may sound unsexy compared to a whirlwind, love-at-first-sight moment, but the results have the potential to last much longer than a ninety-minute movie. Not only that, but the sustained, concentrated effort of building a relationship puts a whole different spin on

"When you know, you know." Because you *will* know, for real, whether or not this is the person for you.

"So how do I do it?" says Dana.

I smile. "I thought you'd never ask."

## Dating from a New Angle

Dana is at a critical juncture in her dating journey: she's failed at love enough times that she's willing to try something radically different.

This is my favorite place to start.

I agree to advise her with the next person she meets through a dating app—but only if she does things my way. First, she's going to select someone who doesn't fit her usual mold. Profession is irrelevant; instead, I want Dana to pick someone whose profile makes her smile. Once she's found a good candidate, she has one job: date 'em 'til you hate 'em.

"Like, *hate* hate 'em?" says Dana.

"Of course not," I reply with a chuckle. "That's just to get your attention. What I really mean is that you will continue dating this person, no matter what, until you are 100 percent sure they are not for you—and never will be."

"But how will I know if I'm sure?"

Oh, if I had a dollar for every time I was asked this question. I'd cruise to Cyprus with my family on our three private yachts: his, hers, and one for the kids.

Pay attention to what Dana is asking: how will she *know* she's sure?

How will you know you're sure? Well . . . when you're sure, you're *sure*. And if you don't know that you're sure, you are in fact *not* sure—and you should keep dating.

Dating is not what most people, including Dana, think it is. They see it as a mental merry-go-round, using minute, superficial shreds of information (and their own projections) to predict the future of the relationship. They become so busy trying to figure out where the relationship is going that they forget to actually build one.

"But isn't it my responsibility to figure out if this relationship will work for me?" Dana counters.

"Nope," I say. "At least, not right away." When done right, dating is simply gathering information. Think of it like a scientist conducting an experiment: they collect objective data, then draw a conclusion. The same applies here. You have to take enough time to get to know a person, *then* use your powers of analysis to make a sound decision.

Coming to know and understand someone is a slow, focused process. It's not something you can accomplish in a date or two. In fact, it takes at least five dates—dates in which you actively try to build a human-to-human connection—to even begin scratching the surface of who they might be, and who they might be with you.

That is why, I tell Dana, she will commit to a minimum of five dates with her next candidate. She is not allowed to break up with him until the allotted five-date mark; in fact, she can make no decisions or even *think* about the relationship until after date five.

"How do I not think about it?" Dana exclaims. "That's basically all I do while I'm going out with them."

My point exactly.

Trying to figure out your relationship before you actually have one is the mental equivalent of chasing your own tail. I see people do it all the time. They make themselves so dizzy, so wracked with anxiety, that it's impossible to make sense of anything. They complicate simple situations, stay with the wrong person out of fear of making a mistake, or bail on a potentially great relationship because it's All. Too. Much.

We want to avoid this. Overthinking is what gets daters into trouble, so if Dana is going to successfully date 'em 'til you hate 'em, she needs to (temporarily) put her brain on pause. For these first five dates, she's going to follow one of my golden rules: assume this person is your future spouse until proven otherwise.

This totally changes the energy of a date.

Instead of analyzing, processing, and dissecting every moment, she's going to observe and listen. She's going to be genuinely excited to try to get to know the other person, and to let him get to know her as well. If he quickly proves he's *not* spouse material, she'll move on to the next, knowing she's one step closer than she was before. That's it.

"So what happens after five dates if I'm still not sure?" she asks.

"When in doubt," I say, "go out."

## Hands-Off Dating

Before she gets started, I add one more proviso to the experiment: no touching for the first five dates.

Dana's response: crickets.

This is to be expected.

In our culture, physical touch is *de rigeur*. Whether it be a handshake in business, hugging a new acquaintance, or greeting your bestie with a breezy kiss on the cheek, touch is not only customary, it's expected.

Why?

Because touch creates connection. The second your body touches another's, a bond forms—for better or worse. Think about it: if you accidentally bump into someone on a crowded subway car, what's your first reaction? If you're like most people, you offer your apologies and conspicuously draw away. This is because, on a subconscious level, you've initiated a relationship. Apologizing is your way of telling them it was unintentional, because if you don't, you know that the connection will linger well after the physical contact is over. Something of you will be left behind—and not in a good way.

If this is the case with a stranger on a train, imagine the impact that touch has on your dating life. From the moment you share even a simple handshake, a relationship has begun. An intention is communicated. The mind and heart begin to fire.

Now imagine you bring kissing or intimacy into the picture.

See where I'm going with this?

When you're just beginning to build a relationship, touch is often more of an obstacle than a help. If you introduce it without taking the time to develop an emotional bond, you can trick yourself into believing there's a deeper connection than there is. It's why, even after dating someone for weeks, months, or even years, a person may think they share real intimacy with their partner when, in reality, they might not know them at all. I've met people in unsatisfying and even destructive relationships who are unable to see it because physical touch has them in such a strong hold. Or worse, they do see it, but they can't find the strength to extricate themselves.

I'm not saying these people are foolish or weak; they're just human. Our bodies and minds are designed to respond to physical contact this way. That's what touch is *for*. It's the reason a lover's passionate kisses feel so magical, and hugs from a loving parental figure feel like home. But like all powerful forces, touch is most potent when it's used in the right time and place.

Which is not during the first five dates.

"But if I don't touch them," Dana asks, "won't they think I'm, you know, a prude?"

I hear this. In the Western world, people who refrain from touch risk being labeled cold, arrogant, a prude, or even a germaphobe. If handled incorrectly, not touching can sometimes do more harm than good. That said, we are also lucky enough to live in the twenty-first century, when diversity and alternative perspectives are (ideally) celebrated. Most people are happy to respect your boundaries, even ones they're unaccustomed to, if they're communicated with kindness and courtesy.

"And if they push back," I say, "it will tell you a lot about who they are."

Dana sighs. "Listen, Aleeza, with all due respect, I know you're an Orthodox Jew, and I know that the no-touching-while-dating thing—what do you call it again?"

"*Shomer negiah.*"

"Right, that."

I laugh.

"I know that's a big part of the Orthodox world," Dana continues. "But I'm not Orthodox. I'm not even religious. I live in the regular world."

Dana's shoulders creep toward her ears; she's anxious that she might have offended me. In fact, the opposite is true. Although as a matchmaker I work with an exclusively Jewish clientele, most of them aren't religious. In fact, many of them identify as agnostics or atheists. My mission as a dating coach is to help my clients find love, period, end of sentence, no matter where they fall on the Jewish spectrum. Still, some of my nonreligious clients have the same thoughts as Dana—many of them even suspect I'm on a crusade to make them Orthodox—but not all of them have the guts to say it directly to my face.

I like this about her.

"I'm not telling you about *shomer negiah* so that you'll be more like me," I assure her. "You don't have to be religious to do it. This isn't even *about* religion. It's about clarity. I want to remove every single obstacle that might block you from finding your person, and I want you to be absolutely sure when you've found him. Holding off on touching is the single most effective way to ensure this happens."

"Right, but . . . how will I know if it works in the bedroom if I don't, you know, try it out?"

This is another one of those yacht-funding questions. A vast majority of my clients come in with missile-gauge focus on sexual compatibility. They want to know right away that things will go smoothly in the bedroom—otherwise, they're out. Actually, they're selling themselves short. Going to bed with someone you're just getting to know is like reading the third page of a novel. The writing could be great. You might really enjoy it so far. But it's nothing compared to reading the last chapter, after you've spent hours savoring the prose, falling in love with the charac-ters, and getting swept away by the plot. Your investment elevates the act of reading from simply enjoyable to something profound and even life changing. The same can be said for couples who have put in the time to build a living, breathing relationship. Even if the mechanics of intimacy aren't absolutely perfect, the emo-tional bond they've built upgrades the experience to a level they could never have achieved in the beginning—a level they might have missed entirely if they'd gotten physical too early.

"Have you ever heard of Tantra?" I ask.

Dana's eyes fly open.

I laugh. "Apparently, you have." And apparently, she never expected an Orthodox woman to brandish the word in front of her.

For the people in the back, the yogic tradition of Tantra weaves together physical and spiritual experience, with the belief that both can mutually enrich each other. This includes the act of sex. The classic teaching of Tantra is that when you allow sexual energy to build up between you and your partner, your erotic experience, when it finally culminates, becomes more intense and connective.

"The longer you wait, the better it is," I say. "In other words, wait five dates."

(Like most rules, there are exceptions to this one. The no-touching rule can be adapted, for example, if you see that the relationship is at risk of drifting into the "friend zone." Sometimes, leveling up the physical connection keeps things from veering off course. Sometimes, though, it does the opposite, so tread lightly. If lack of physical touch triggers a past trauma, prevents you from truly opening up, or is something so deeply important to you that you couldn't imagine bonding without it, I understand. But even then, do so with both eyes open.

Remember, while this may be a hard-and-fast rule for *me*, you are free to apply it at your comfort level—just as long as you don't go all or nothing. Some people commit to no kissing for the first five dates, or for the first three. Some incorporate touching but commit to ten dates instead of five. Others commit fully in the beginning and adjust as they go. The only wrong way to do this is not to do it at all. Whenever you decide to move forward with touching, pace yourself. Start slowly and let the connection build as much as possible first.)

Dana shrugs. "I'm willing to give it a shot. But . . . what happens after the fifth date?"

"That's up to you."

"You mean, I can just . . ."

I chuckle. "I'm not signing off on anything, but you can assume I'll look the other way—twenty-four hours after date five is over."

Dana grins. "It's a deal."

## Date One

The first time Dana sees Will, her initial thought is: *meh.*

It's not that he's bad looking: Will has a thick head of hair and a lovely smile. It's just that, in a pair of jeans, a casual button-down, and glasses, he's so different from the dressed-to-impress men she's dated in the past. He's simpler. More down-to-earth. But that was why Dana swiped right on the dating app in the first place (with a little encouragement from me). A professor of social psychology, Will's profile had the perfect balance of humor and heart. His social media feed was a playlist of various unique destinations he's visited for research and pleasure—Kenya, Peru, New Zealand—interspersed with insightful quotes and pictures of Will with family and friends. If the product matched the advertisement, Will looked like a good guy.

And yet, as she approaches him at a dimly lit trattoria in SoHo, Dana can't help but notice how unexcited she is. *This relationship is already dead in the water,* she mentally grumbles. Then Dana remembers that she doesn't have to decide that now; all she has to do is be open and observe.

Will greets her warmly, moving to hug her. Having anticipated that this might happen, Dana clasps her hands together in front of her chest and smiles. "It's *so* nice to meet you. Forgive me for not hugging you. I'm trying something that was recommended to me by a friend of mine and going hands-free for the first five dates."

"Interesting," Will says, sounding more curious than disconcerted. "Does that mean no touching at all?"

"It does. I hope that's okay."

"Sure," he says. "Is it alright if I pull out your chair?"

Dana smiles again. "Of course. Thank you."

Point one for Will.

Over wine and gnocchi, they jump right into talking about their careers. Dana tells Will that she promised herself she'd make partner at her firm by thirty-five, which is why she's in the office late almost every night (she plans on heading back there after this date). Even during the COVID-19 lockdown, her hours didn't change.

"Impressive," Will replies. "You must love what you do."

Dana thinks about it. "I like my work, but what I love is being good at it. If I wasn't, I don't think the sacrifices I've made would be worth it."

"So, then, really, you could do anything, as long as you do it successfully."

This stirs something in Dana. She's never considered that before.

"Is being successful important to you?" Dana asks.

"Yes," Will continues, "as long as it's *my* measure of success. For you, it's making partner in your firm, litigating prestigious cases, and, I assume, making great money. And you're doing it, which is fantastic. When I first got into academia, I had big dreams to publish books, conduct groundbreaking research, and teach at universities around the world. And I've done some of those things. Not all, but some. In academia, you're always expected to do more—you know, publish or perish—so even though I was technically successful, I never felt like I was. Then things changed."

Dana leans forward, curious. "What happened?"

"I realized that I really love being a professor. I love my students. I love my assistants. It wasn't about the books or the research or the tenure. Those things are still valuable to me, but they don't bring me joy the way teaching does. And I get to do it *every day*. That's when I realized I'm already a success." Will shakes his head and laughs. "Sorry, I didn't mean for that to turn into a lecture. Hazards of dating an academic."

Dana shakes her head. "I liked what you said. It was . . . inspiring."

"Or didactic. Depends on who you ask."

"No, I know didactic. If I disagreed with my ex about anything, he'd talk at me for *hours* about how I was wrong."

Will looks sheepish. "I've been guilty of something similar."

"I assume you've kicked the habit?"

"I have," he says with a chuckle, "because I don't want to stay single forever."

Dana laughs. "Me, neither."

For the rest of the meal, the conversation (and wine) flows easily. Dana realizes that, without the pressure of anticipating whether or not Will is going to kiss her or having to puzzle out where things are going, she can just be present. In fact, this is the first time she has ever been on a date and felt—dare she say it?—*relaxed.*

After Will pays the check, he walks Dana out of the restaurant and hails her a cab. "It was a pleasure," he says. "Can we do it again?"

Dana hesitates. Although she's had a nice time, she doubts that this is going anywhere. This guy is barely even her type. And don't professors get the summers off? How can she have a relationship with someone who—

She stops herself. Dana has committed to five dates. She's promised not to make any decisions until then. Which means she has no choice but to say, "I'd love to."

For a brief moment, he moves his arms as if to hug her, then stops himself. "Right. I forgot. Well . . . consider yourself hugged."

Dana laughs. "Thanks."

Overall, this first date was promising. Despite her lack of initial excitement about Will, Dana kept her mind open instead of lamenting a lost "meet-cute" moment. This is important, as we will see; not feeling butterflies in the beginning might just mean the caterpillars need more time.

In my opinion, Dana handled her no-touching boundary like a pro. She was courteous and direct without being scraping—though I would have been happier if she hadn't asked Will if it was okay with him. Frankly, Will's opinion about it is irrelevant. If this is what makes Dana comfortable, Will is free to either take it or leave it (and, I must say, he took it like a *mensch*). However, I also understand the impulse to soften the blow when setting a boundary like this one; it can be off-putting if not handled right. But because Dana did such a great job right off the bat, I don't think it was necessary.

However, she fell into a danger zone after Will confessed his past habit of lecturing people. This was a vulnerable moment for him; Dana would have done well to show him empathy and encouragement, even if what he said triggered her. Instead, she told him how much it bothered her when her ex had done the same thing, then not-so-subtly hinted to Will that he'd better get his act together. Clearly, this was a pain point that caused her to react out of fear. Lucky for her, Will took it in stride. With someone else, it could have backfired. In my experience, people are always more open to growth and change when they feel safe; the opposite happens when they feel threatened. If Dana ideally wants Will to learn how to be a more attentive and giving partner, she'll have to practice positive communication skills.

One more point: *Please, for the love of all that is Pure and Holy, do not bash your exes and do not talk about them at all on the first date.* Notice how I italicized that? It's because I *really mean it.* There is nothing less attractive (and more revealing) than talking smack about someone you used to date with someone you hope to have a relationship with. You make it easy for them to picture you, months down the road, doing the same thing to them. A new relationship is like a blank canvas; don't ruin it by slinging mud. Just to be safe, avoid talking about exes entirely until at least three dates in. Keep your focus on the person in front of you, not the one you've left behind.

On a positive note, all the points to Will for paying the bill. Call me old-fashioned, but I believe that men should pay for at least the first few dates. Generally speaking, women inherently have a stronger need to feel cared for and provided for than men do; covering the bill lays the groundwork for women to feel safe and trusting toward their date. That said, no matter who pays, he or she should cover the entire bill. In my view, splitting the bill splits the connection. Whether it's one dollar or a hundred dollars, paying for someone communicates your investment in them (literally and figuratively) and tells them you value their time and company. It makes you a unit, instead of two separate individuals. This isn't a lifelong commitment, and the same person doesn't have to pay each time. But the gesture goes a long way toward opening two hearts to a new relationship.

We'll also commend Dana for keeping her mind open. She never would have considered a guy like Will before, let alone gone out with him. If it wasn't for this experiment, there's no way she would have made it past (or even through) this first date. Good for her for keeping to her commitment and not dismissing Will for what he isn't. Now she gets to discover who he is.

Let's see how it goes.

## Date Three

Fast-forward to Will and Dana's third date, which starts with Sunday brunch. At least, it's supposed to. But just two minutes after sitting down, Dana closes her menu. "I changed my mind," she says.

Will looks up, intrigued. "About . . . ?"

"I spent the whole day yesterday inside because of the rain, and it's so gorgeous out now. Do you think we could take a walk instead?"

He peers out the window, then back at Dana, and shrugs. "Sure."

"Really?"

"Why not?"

"We had plans . . ."

"I once had plans to live in a monastery. Now I live in Flatbush. Plans change."

Dana laughs. "Sure you don't mind?"

"Not at all. Let's go."

Ditching the restaurant and grabbing coffee and croissants from a nearby bakery, Will and Dana begin their walk around New York City. They pick through a farmers market, pet dogs at an outdoor adoption event, admire the vibrant colors of a flower show, and watch skateboarders wipe out on ramps. Dana drinks in springtime in New York, and is grateful to Will for being so flexible. She's surprised by how easy it is with him, the natural rhythm of their conversation, and how much they laugh together.

*He feels like an old friend,* she thinks.

As the sun sets, they find themselves crossing the bridge into Brooklyn, where Will lives, and realize they're famished.

"You like tacos?" Will asks.

"Is that a rhetorical question?"

He takes her to a hole-in-the-wall taqueria where Will promises they have the best guacamole outside of Mexico. Dana is thrilled to discover that he's right.

With tired legs and full bellies, Dana walks Will to his door—nine hours after their date began.

"Thanks for taking a walk with me," Dana says.

"It was," Will replies, "an excellent idea."

She eyes him. "Did you really want to live in a monastery?"

"Once upon a time. Then I found out they don't serve tacos . . ."

Dana laughs.

This date is proof that sometimes, a change of plans can change everything. It's likely that if Dana and Will had stuck with brunch, they would have had a nice time. But I truly believe that it would not have been as special a day for them as this one was. It began with Dana, who listened to what she wanted and spoke up. Something about Will made her feel comfortable enough to suggest a change of plans, and her instinct was right: he was more than happy to accommodate her. This speaks volumes about Dana's ability to be vulnerable and to ask for what she needs, and for Will's readiness to accommodate her.

I have only one complaint about this date: it went on too long. In my book, you stick with fives: five dates, a maximum of five hours per date, and no more than five days between dates. While the idea of a long date sounds romantic, you don't want to spend all your energy and excitement in one shot. Better to call it a night early so you can look forward to seeing each other again. At the same time, you want to keep the momentum going by not letting too much time lapse between dates. Remember that we're looking for clarity; too much activity, too fast or too little progression in too long a stretch can throw you off balance. Sticking with fives keeps the relationship humming along at a manageable pace and carries you smoothly to a clear outcome. If it's meant to work out, you'll know pretty quickly. And if it isn't, you can move on, pronto.

## Date Four

The morning of their fourth date, Dana calls Will with some bad news: "I'bbbb—ah . . . ah . . . ah . . . chooo!"

"Sick?" Will offers.

Dana groans, and sneezes again. She begrudgingly recites her symptoms: fever, chills, headache. No one likes being sick, but Dana resents it. It's harder to get work done.

"I guess we're not going out tonight."

"I'bb sorry, Will."

"Don't be sorry. Just get some sleep."

A few hours later, there's a knock at Dana's door. In the hallway, she finds a bouquet of flowers and a bag with a note attached to it: *Some essentials for the patient, hot off the stove. Pour yourself a bowl, get back into bed, and call me. Feel good, Will.*

Inside the bag, Dana discovers a large, warm container of golden chicken soup.

"Oh by gosh!" she exclaims.

Following Will's directions, she warms some soup in a bowl and takes a sip.

It's instant, heavenly relief. She might even be able to go back to working on the contract she had to review.

Immediately, Dana calls Will. "I can't believe you bade me chiggen soup!"

"I made *me* chicken soup. But I'm a nice guy, so I decided to share with you."

Dana laughs.

"Are you in bed?"

"Yeah, why?"

"Turn on Netflix. We're going to watch *Singin' in the Rain*."

"Like, the musical?"

"Is there a different one?"

Dana hesitates for a moment. She has work to do. But watching a movie with Will sounds nice. "I've never seen it."

"Well, I won't comment on your deprived childhood, but I will tell you that whenever I was sick, my mom made fresh chicken soup, wrapped me up in a blanket, and we watched *Singin' in the Rain* together. It is, hands down, the best movie of all time. So today is your lucky day."

That settles it. The contract can wait. Dana is surprised by how wonderful it feels to be cared for this way. Though Will may not be there in person, his presence on the other end of the phone brings her profound relief, as if she's finally found something precious she'd thought she'd lost. And it hits her: Dana hasn't only wanted someone who would support her career; she's longed for a partner who supports *her*.

The realization is so stunning, it might have knocked Dana off her feet if she wasn't already sitting down.

It does feel like her lucky day.

"Ready?" Will asks.

Dana smiles into the phone. "Ready."

Oh. My.

While I feel bad that Dana is sick, I love that Will grabbed this opportunity to take care of her, because it afforded Dana a life-changing revelation. Recognizing her need to be supported on a human level, not just as a professional, Dana has opened herself up to a deeper sense of who she is. Her career is important, but it's not everything. Will's investment in Dana, the person, has woken her up to the value of investing in herself.

Will's gesture was thoughtful and kind—two qualities I love to hear about in my clients' prospective partners. More importantly, he did it because he wanted to, not because he felt obligated or was trying to impress Dana. The experience of being lovingly cared for as a kid was so meaningful to him that he was excited to share it with her. This tells us volumes about his ability to show love without holding back or expecting anything in return.

Hollywood romances can mislead us into believing that love is born through sweeping, dramatic gestures: Jack saving Rose from falling off the *Titanic*; Noah hanging from a Ferris wheel to ask Ally on a date; Patrick serenading Kat with "Can't Take My Eyes off of You" in front of the entire soccer team; or Mr. Darcy professing his love to Elizabeth in the rain. These moments have merit, but when it comes to building a relationship, they're about as strong as Scotch tape. It's the small, quiet wins, when one subtly shows up for the other, that have the power to cement two people together over time. It didn't take much for Will to bring soup to Dana, but in terms of their relationship, it just might have been a game-changer.

## Date Five

On their fifth date, Will and Dana head to Little Italy for the Feast of San Gennaro. Though both have lived in the city for years, neither have been to the festival before. They weave among the throngs of people, taking in the twinkling lights, the music, the symphony of voices and accents. They agree, biting into cannolis, that it was worth the wait.

There's something magical in the evening air. As a quartet of guitarists strikes up a romantic melody, Will grabs a broom from a nearby restaurant and dances with it across the cobblestones like Fred Astaire.

Dana cracks up. "You're crazy!"

"Well, I can't dance with you, so this is the next best thing!"

People gather to watch Will, laughing along with Dana. She loves how carefree and unselfconscious he is, how fluidly his body moves. It makes him look sexy. At the end of the song, Will dips the broom deeply to a round of applause. He bows to the crowd, then to the band. Then he grins at Dana.

She's surprised to feel her heart jump.

"You're a great dancer!" she says, as Will tosses a few bills into the quartet's open guitar case.

"That's four years of ballroom dancing lessons, thank you very much," he says. "I had to take an extracurricular in high school, and the chess club was full. Then I ended up liking it."

"I'm jealous," Dana confides. "I'm hopeless at dancing."

"You just haven't found the right partner," he replies breezily. "When your strengths complement each other, you can fuse them together into one motion. It's a give-and-take thing; sometimes, one person leads the dance, then the other person takes over."

She can tell by the way Will looks at her that he's talking about more than just dancing. He's describing a relationship in which both of them support each other.

"I want to kiss you," he says, leaning in close.

Dana smiles. "I want you to kiss me, too."

"It's still the fifth date."

"Aleeza says she starts looking the other way twenty-four hours after this date is over."

"So we'll both go home right now . . ." Will begins.

Dana laughs.

". . . and I will see you in twenty-four hours."

Dana calls me, giggling.

"So I guess you don't hate him?" I ask.

"This is crazy! On our first date, I was sure this was going nowhere. But he just . . . grew on me. Now I can't believe I almost dumped him!"

I'm not the type of person to say "I told you so," but *come on*. Imagine if Dana had bailed on Will after that first date (or ruled him out completely!). If she hadn't committed to five dates, there's no doubt she would have done exactly that. But because she stuck it out, she discovered someone truly special.

I once had a client tell me, when she decided to marry the man she'd been dating, "He's everything I never knew I always wanted." Something similar has happened to Dana. The more time she spent with Will, the clearer she saw qualities she values in a person, as opposed to fixating on one detail and missing the person entirely. No matter what the future of this relationship turns out to be, I don't imagine that Dana will date the same way ever again.

## CHAPTER ONE TIP

**The Five, Five, and Five Rule:** *Five dates, no more than five hours per date, and no more than five days between dates*

Why?

**Five Dates:** Plenty of people aren't their best on a first date. By committing to at least five dates, you're giving yourself (and your date!) a chance to put your best self forward.

**Five Hours:** As P. T. Barnum said, "Always leave 'em wanting more." Capping a date at five hours prevents both parties from getting tapped out and keeps the spark alive.

**Five Days:** If you've got something good going, the last thing you want to do is lose the momentum by letting too much time lapse between dates.

CHAPTER TWO

# High-Quality Humans

Josh grew up watching "tough guys" on TV: Rambo, He-Man, GI Joe, Teenage Mutant Ninja Turtles, Power Rangers— heroes who were strong and quick and always saved the day. He collected dozens of action figures and spent hours playing with them, protecting LEGO cities and the honor of damsels in distress (usually a Barbie stolen from his sister's room). He loved the charge of power he felt from vanquishing enemies and winning the heart of a beautiful woman, even if it was just in his imagination. As he got older, he started hitting the gym, shaping his physique to match that of his heroes—and getting the female attention his heroes got. Yet, over the next twenty years, despite a series of monogamous relationships, Josh never found The One. Now he laments that his rad bod is looking more like a dad bod, and he is starting to lose hope.

"None of my relationships last longer than a couple of months," he tells me. "I'm tired of having to start over, over and over again." This is a familiar anthem with my clients: exhausted by the dating grind, they just want to be on the other side of finding love.

"Why do you think it doesn't last?" I ask.

"I know why it doesn't: the spark keeps dying."

"Tell me more about the spark."

"In the beginning, it's magic," Josh says, smiling. "Everything is exciting—especially in bed. All I can think about is being with her. And it's a relief, because I feel like I've *finally* found my person. But then, it just goes . . . flat. The magic disappears."

"What made it disappear?"

"I guess she wasn't the right person."

"So, Josh," I prod, "what kind of person is the right person?"

He has no answer.

*This* is where Josh has gotten himself stuck. In reality, he isn't dating; he's chasing the high of attraction. The "spark" he thinks is the beginning of love is really just a mixture of lust and the ego hit of a woman's admiration. So he jumps into a physical connection without building emotional intimacy, assuming that the connection will grow naturally if he's with the right person. That's why it's only a matter of time until the "spark" dies.

If Josh wants to find *real* love, it's time for him to drop his quest for the elusive "spark" and start looking for a flesh-and-blood person.

"And not just any person," I insist. "What you want is a high-quality human."

## What Is a High-Quality Human?

In the summer of 2006, a twenty-year-old tank commander named Ron prepared himself for an upcoming late-night raid. Ron was worried, partly because of the raid, but also because his brother's wedding was scheduled to take place in three weeks. Ron's brother had overcome a difficult past, so for him and his family, the celebration was twofold and highly anticipated. Though not religious at the time, Ron offered up a prayer: "God, listen, I don't know what you have in the cards for me, but if you kill me, this wedding might not happen. Just injure me or something, because my brother has to get married."

God must have heard his prayer, because in the middle of the raid, a concrete building collapsed on Ron. The tank driver, Ron's friend Yaneev, helped dig him out for helicopter transport to the hospital. There, Ron learned that he had lost the use of his legs due to a spinal cord injury and would spend the rest of his life using a wheelchair. As for Yaneev, he'd been killed by an anti-tank missile after taking Ron's place in the raid.

There are a multitude of ways that Ron could have responded to this course of events. He might have fallen into a depression over being wheelchair-bound at twenty. He could have been plagued by guilt over the death of his friend. He might have stewed in bitterness, self-pity, or a desire for revenge. Or, worst of all, he could have given up on life.

But he did none of these things.

Instead, Ron became an international speaker, executive coach, and musician who inspires people around the world. His talks focus on embracing life, making the most of opportunities, overcoming fear and doubt, and appreciating the gift of being alive. He's competed in the Eurovision Song Contest and trained leaders at companies like Boeing, General Electric, IBM, NASA, and the FBI. His charisma is electric, magnetic, unstoppable; he travels internationally, drives himself wherever he wishes to go (popping in and out of his wheelchair with a dancer's coordination), and lights up every room he enters with his upbeat energy, megawatt smile, and curly man bun.

But that's not all. When I asked him what kind of woman he was looking for, this is what he said: "I don't really care about what she looks like. If she sparkles on the inside, if she has drive, passion, and desire to grow, then whatever is on the outside will be hot."

I've met thousands of singles in my life, and Ron is the only person who has ever said this to me.

All I could think was: *If I had a daughter the right age, this guy would be next in line.*

Ron is what I call a high-quality human.

High-quality humans are the gold nuggets in the mine of dating. They are the crème de la crème of people. They are the

Coliseum, the Mona Lisa, a Mozart concerto, a Shakespeare sonnet, or a Stradivarius in human form. They are what you want in a partner. If you happen to find one, I absolutely forbid you to let them go.

High-quality humans are evolved and well-developed. While self-aware, they don't focus inward; instead, they constantly seek ways to experience, interact, engage, and give to the world. They're conscientious and thoughtful, uninterested in being the center of the universe but excited to be a part of it. They don't care about being impressed; they want to be *involved*. These people usually have hobbies, passions, aspirations, pet subjects, ideas—and they *do* something with them. HQHs are open to experience; these are people who say "Yes!" to life. Instead of running from their imperfections, they embrace them, using their mistakes as launchpads for growth. With others, they're respectful, compassionate, and empathetic. They don't demand that you meet them where they are; they want to understand who *you* are. The difference between HQHs and regular civilians comes down to this: they hold themselves to a higher standard than they do others, instead of the other way around.

Many HQHs are dynamic extroverts like Ron. These are often diamonds who have been polished by pressure and hardship, which they use to fuel their thoughts and feelings into action. The second you meet them, you know they're something special—in Hollywood terms, you'd call them blockbusters. However, there are plenty of introverted, "sleeper" HQHs, too. They're not as flashy, so it's harder to see at first. But it's only a matter of time until their positive attitude, humility, and kindness work their magic.

One example of these "sleeper" HQHs is a former client of mine, a medical researcher named Dave. Reserved and shy, it was hard to tell, when you first met him, if he even had a *personality*. But with a little prodding, I discovered that he was passionate about pottery. Dave grew up in Texas, a state that worships sports (especially football)—hell on earth for a kid with osteogenesis imperfecta, or brittle bone disease. Due to his condition, which caused his bones to fracture easily, Dave could go nowhere near a basketball court, football field, or baseball diamond. In a community obsessed with athleticism, he was given few opportunities to shine. Over time, Dave started to wonder if there was anything shiny about him. Then one day, his art teacher brought her pottery wheel into class. From the second Dave sat in front of it, it was clear he was a natural. While the other kids went too rough and made messes of their clay, Dave's delicate movements, which he'd developed to protect his body, were perfectly calibrated to coax the clay just the way he wanted. His teacher gushed about Dave's "magic hands." From that day on, he was hooked. Now a master potter, in his spare time Dave teaches classes for children and teens who, like him, just want a chance to shine.

Not all HQHs are meant to change the course of history. Some of them don't even know how to change a tire. But spend enough time with one, and they will absolutely change you.

Most people don't recognize a high-quality human when they see one. Most of the time, they're so fixated on what they think they want, they miss these gorgeous specimens entirely. Even worse, they might have one right in front of them and not even recognize it. If so, they have missed the opportunity of a lifetime. The best dating advice I could possibly give to anyone who *really* wants a long-lasting, satisfying relationship is to forget everything you think you want and find yourself a high-quality human.

But here's the hitch: it takes one to know one.

"In other words," I tell Josh, "if you want a high-quality human as your partner, you'll need to become one yourself."

Josh's eyebrows shoot up. "Listen, I'm a decent guy, but I'm no one special. I'm not a war hero. I've never done pottery in my life. How do I become a high-quality human?"

"Are you human?"

"Pretty sure."

"Great. Then you qualify."

The good news is that no matter who you are or what you've been through, anyone can become a high-quality human. In fact, I believe the entire point of our lives is to do just that. All it takes is becoming the best, most whole, and most alive version of yourself. When we nurture our gifts and learn from our setbacks, we have the opportunity to leave the world a little better than we found it. This is a lifelong journey, but once you get started, you're in the company of the best people. Most HQHs don't always begin as HQHs. Many of them have to do some serious healing to let go of the past and ground themselves in reality, to acknowledge themselves and their circumstances as they are and not how they think they should be. So many people lose years trying to fit their lives to a mold that doesn't fit them, then wonder why they're always frustrated (especially in love). If you buy the pieces for an IKEA dresser, you wouldn't ignore the directions and try to build a bike. This is true for you, too. Find out what you're made of, then follow the directions. You'll inevitably discover treasures inside yourself and watch a beautiful life grow around you when you live according to your own design.

This is what it means to be a high-quality human.

Josh has the makings of a high-quality human: he's wise, insightful, and open to growth. He's also clearly willing to admit where he needs work—hence his visit with me. Knowing his old ways of dating have failed him, he agrees to try the date 'em 'til you hate 'em experiment with the next person he meets through a dating app—though, he informs me, "there is no way on God's green earth that I can hold off on touching her for five dates." The look of horror on his face makes me burst into laughter.

"Josh, relax. I'm not asking you to be celibate forever. It's just five dates."

"That could take, like, *weeks*."

"You know what they say about Rome, and that was just a bunch of buildings. A relationship is much more challenging to get off the ground."

"I'll make you a deal," he says. "I'll *consider* not kissing her for the first three."

"I'll take it. Just remember that this isn't about how you feel, but who she is. And, of course, who you are, too."

## Date One

In a quiet cafe in Center City, Josh waits for Emma, a Philadelphia city planner. He arrived ten minutes early, so he has time to check out Emma's profile one more time: lovely picture, clever write-up. *Here's hoping this woman is who she says she is,* Josh thinks.

Emma enters the cafe ten minutes after their meeting time, rolling a neon pink Schwinn bicycle beside her. As she removes her helmet and shakes out her hair, Josh's mouth almost falls open: her profile picture does not do her justice. This woman is *stunning*: lush auburn hair, wide green eyes, full lips, an hourglass silhouette. He immediately feels his temperature rise a few degrees. His heart starts beating a little faster. Josh relishes the excitement—but reminds himself not to be misled. As good as it feels to be excited about someone, this is no longer Josh's end goal.

As he hugs Emma hello, Josh finds himself hyperaware of even the most innocent physical contact. The subtle hum of energy between their bodies makes his blood spike, and he finds himself liking her even more.

"How was traffic?" she asks.

"Not great, but definitely worth it."

He smiles.

She smiles back.

They chat about their backgrounds—she grew up in Los Angeles, but moved to Philadelphia for graduate school and stayed; he is a Philly boy born and bred—and their interests.

As part of her work, Emma has recently returned from a whirl-wind trip to Hong Kong, Amsterdam, Rio de Janeiro, and San Francisco, all considered some of the world's most pedestrian-friendly cities.

"Growing up in LA, I couldn't walk anywhere," Emma recalls. "I didn't realize how much it affected my mental health until I moved here. Now I know it's because LA is designed for cars, not people. That's why I went into urban planning; I want to make walkable and bikeable cities the norm. They're better for people, and the planet."

"Is that what you're doing for Philly? Making it more walkable?"

"I'm trying to," she says with a chuckle. "Right now, I'm developing a sensory-friendly playground not far from the zoo. Not *exactly* on track for my vision, but it is for the kids."

This is the first date in which Josh has done so little talking. Usually, he pilots the conversation, steering it toward opportunities to flatter and flirt, warming his date up to an invitation home with him. But tonight, knowing that his job is to simply gather information, and having committed not to make a move, he really listens to Emma.

"Do you like kids?" he asks.

"Love them. You?"

Josh's first impulse is to agree out of a desire to please her. It's something he's done many times: contorting himself to appeal to a woman he wants. But since he's trying things differently this time, he decides to go with honesty: "I don't know."

Josh doesn't anticipate how vulnerable telling the truth would feel. He launches into damage control: "It's not that I don't like kids, I just don't have a lot of experience with them."

"I don't, either," Emma says. "When I'm stuck on something for the park, I call one of my mom friends and pick her brain. I'm going to be in big trouble when I have kids of my own."

Josh notices her use of the word *when*, not *if*.

"Do you want kids?" she asks.

He takes a thoughtful sip of water. He's gone this far; he might as well stick with the truth. "Honestly, I could go either way. If my wife wanted kids, I'd be open to it. But if she didn't, I think I'd be okay, too."

Though Josh offers to pay, Emma insists on splitting the check. Then they head to a gelato place that lets you try before you buy. They spend ten minutes taste-testing every flavor before Josh asks her if she wants to share their two favorites.

"No, thanks," she says. "I don't like sharing."

*Fair,* Josh thinks, despite his disappointment. *Maybe it's a germ thing.*

After they've polished off their gelatos, Emma walks Josh to his car.

"I'd like to see you again," Josh says.

"I'd like that, too."

This is the moment when, any other night, he might have tried to kiss her. Instead, he hugs her again. "Can I drive you?"

"No, thanks. Suzie—" she pats her Schwinn with affection "—and I want to take the long way home."

Josh watches with a smile as she mounts the bike and rides away in a blur of neon pink.

Overall, I think Josh and Emma's first date was a win.

First, there was Josh's immediate attraction. This is not guaranteed when you meet someone for the first time, and it makes my job (and his) a lot easier. Of course, attraction can be cultivated (more on that later), but when it happens right off the bat, it's a nice boost to get the relationship off the ground.

The danger is assuming that attraction guarantees a great relationship, a mistake that Josh has made in the past. This is why it's excellent that he's keeping physical contact to a minimum. The excitement of attraction coupled with the electricity of touch would probably have distracted him. For the same reason, Josh gets extra points for letting the conversation run its natural course instead of trying to spice it up. Without the focus on taking Emma home, Josh could actually get to know her.

Kudos to Josh, also, for not taking Emma's desire to have her own gelato personally. One of the best pieces of advice I ever heard was, "Don't worry about what other people think of you because they're not thinking of you; they're thinking of themselves." Ninety-nine percent of the things people do, think, and say have everything to do with them and nothing to do with you. People make the mistake of inverting this ratio and then react to the story they've told themselves about it. Josh could have been offended by Emma's "rejection" and assumed she didn't like him. He might have even shut down in response. But as a mature person, he accepted Emma's decision without making it about him.

In this vein, Josh proved himself a master of the art of an old Jewish concept called "judging others for the good." Instead of condemning other people's choices, you can assume they have a good reason for making them. If, for example, someone cuts you off on the highway, it's easy to flip them the bird. But have you considered the possibility that they have a medical emergency or a friend with car trouble? In Josh's case, he opted not to think negatively about Emma and instead guessed that she had an aversion to germs. Whether or not she does isn't the point. The fact that Josh put his effort and imagination toward a positive, healthy outcome is a beautiful reflection on his character. It also afforded him peace of mind.

In my opinion, however, there were two snafus on this date. The first was Emma's insistence on splitting the bill, which, as I've said before, splits the connection. The other, more major bump was that they brought up the subject of kids. In general, I advise my clients to steer clear of hot topics like kids, money, and politics on the first date. These button-pushers can kill a good thing before it starts. Better to get to know a person first so that when these issues come up, they'll be part of a greater, more balanced context. Something that would have been a deal-breaker on date one, for example, might be no big deal on date four. A couple I know named Debbie and Rob have been married for forty years and have four children together. Every election, he votes Republican and she votes Democrat ("We cancel each other out every time," Debbie jokes). Clearly, they have widely divergent political views. But because they built a relationship with each other first, they agree to disagree and enjoy their life together.

(Not to say that some of these topics *won't* be deal-breakers. One person's desire to be a parent, for example, is not compatible with another person's decision to remain childfree. And when it comes to politics, different opinions are one thing, but different core values are another. What we want to avoid, though, is prematurely dismissing someone with real potential based on one factor that, down the road, could be perfectly workable in the relationship.)

However, there was a plus side to the kid conversation: it gave Josh an opportunity to be vulnerable in a way he had never been with a date before. Instead of slipping into people-pleasing, he shared his ambivalence about children with Emma. Josh was lucky that her reaction was accepting and positive, but it also would have been okay if it wasn't. Being authentic from the get-go is one of the most important aspects of building a healthy and satisfying relationship with another person. It's a risk that many people avoid. Hats off to Josh for rising to the occasion.

## Date Three

Josh and Emma spend a Sunday on Jenkinson's Boardwalk at Point Pleasant Beach. This was Emma's suggestion; a product of the West Coast, she's her happiest by the ocean.

As they walk the shoreline, watch salt water taffy stretch in a mechanical puller, and share a bucket of greasy fries, Josh notices that most of their conversation (and all of their activities) revolves around Emma. He doesn't need to be the central topic, but it would be nice if she asked him a bit more about himself. But still, only three dates into the date 'em 'til you hate 'em experiment, Josh is trying not to draw any conclusions just yet. Instead, he digs into the conversation, hoping to unearth some connection points.

At the aquarium, they watch a small colony of penguins scuttling around. Josh reads aloud from a nearby placard: "*'All species of penguins are monogamous and form partnerships that can last from a year to a lifetime. They also exhibit biparental care, with father and mother raising one to two chicks together.'*"

"They make it sound so easy," Emma jokes.

"Maybe it is," says Josh. "Maybe we humans just complicate things."

"That's for sure. Just look at my parents."

"They didn't get along?"

Emma scoffs. "That's putting it mildly. Their marriage was bad, and the divorce was even worse. It was the ugliest game of tug-of-war you've ever seen, and my sisters and I were the rope."

"My parents are divorced, too," Josh says. "But they both got remarried to great people, so it worked out in the end."

"Mine have both been divorced a couple of times. Makes me worry about my odds . . ." Emma laughs.

"Just because your parents got divorced doesn't mean you will."

"I hope so. I like the idea of growing old with someone who really loves me."

Josh's ears perk up at that last sentence. Emma has inadvertently shared her marriage ideal: apparently, it's not sharing a life with a partner, but simply finding someone to love her.

If Emma realizes that she's put him off, she makes no sign of it. They lapse into silence—something which, in general, makes Josh uncomfortable. He has the impulse to start talking again, or to pull Emma to him and kiss her . . . but instead of doing so, he asks himself why.

It's because he's afraid.

Everything seemed perfect on the first date. The chemistry was electric, and Emma has all the right qualities: she's beautiful, smart, fun. But the more he's learning about Emma, the less he likes her. The flip side of Emma's laid-back, California-girl vibe is her inability to commit until the last minute and a tendency to show up late. This doesn't jive with Josh's more regimented, East Coast sensibility. Josh also feels that when he talks, Emma isn't really listening, but waiting for her turn to speak.

There is one thing they do seem to have in common, though: a shared interest in Emma.

He's starting to suspect that Emma is not the person he wants her to be.

In his past relationships, Josh may have noticed potential issues, but he was too distracted by the physical, or by his investment in Happily Ever After, to acknowledge them until much farther down the road. He *really* wants it to work out with Emma, which explains his impulse to kiss her: it's the easiest way to create connection and override his fear of being disappointed again. But now that Josh knows better, he can't bring himself to do it.

Also, to be honest, he's not sure he *wants* to kiss her.

This shocks him more than anything.

The rest of the date goes smoothly enough. Josh wins Emma a teddy bear at one of the game stands and they share hamburgers as the sun sets. At the end of the date, sunburned and sandy, Emma kisses his cheek and invites him up to her apartment.

"Thanks," he says, "but I'm pretty tired."

He's not sure which of them is more surprised.

While this date does leave Josh with some ambivalence about Emma, I still consider it a victory for him.

Josh is starting to date from an entirely new angle; instead of trying to shoehorn Happily Ever After onto the wrong-sized foot, he's actually taking measurements to see if it's even worth trying on. True, he did have the impulse to fabricate a connection with physical touch. In a moment of discomfort, he almost fell back into an old habit. But this time, he refrained and let it teach him a deeper lesson.

I appreciate Josh's concern about Emma, who seems to look at relationships as a solar system, with herself as the sun. But let's try to reserve judgment; we've been *taught* to look at love this way. In our society, being in a relationship is a stamp of validation that you are worthy, wanted, and loveable. Women especially are given the message that their ultimate purpose in life is to find a partner. This is why I've met many, many people with the same perspective. They've flipped their binoculars backward, focusing on how to win someone's affection instead of exploring their own feelings. Then they wonder why they can't find their other half. It's because they're not looking for their other half; they're looking for *themselves*.

There is a significant difference between dating and seeking validation from another person. If you're not sure which one you're doing, ask yourself this: are you more concerned with how *they* feel about *you* or how *you* feel about *them*? If you are looking inward and examining your feelings about the other person, you are dating. If you are preoccupied with their feelings about *you*, you are probably looking for more than just love.

In case no one has ever told you this, allow me: it's no one's job but yours to convince you that you are worthy and good enough. Looking for someone else to do it is an unfair expectation and a disservice to you and anyone you date. If you have fallen into this trap, forgive yourself; it was set long before you even knew to look for it. But now that you know it's there, do whatever it takes to set yourself free. Learn how to give yourself what you need so you can go out and find someone you *want*.

That said, I would caution Josh about giving up on Emma so quickly. Remember, we want to judge for the good. They're only on date three, after all; it's still a tender, vulnerable time. It's possible that Emma was nervous and reverted to a comfortable topic: herself. This doesn't mean she's completely self-centered; she just might need more time to open up. For Josh, this is a challenge to stay put when he discovers a flaw in the person he's dating. To have a real relationship with a high-quality human, he's going to have to get comfortable with imperfections—his own and his partner's. His experience with Emma is excellent practice.

## Date Five

A lifelong sports fan, Josh invites Emma to an event that is quintessentially him: a Philadelphia Phillies game. Emma doesn't know much about baseball, but since he's already bought the tickets, she's willing to give it a shot.

Josh spends a good part of the first inning giving her a rundown of the players and some history of the team, but she's barely listening. "Do they have to play the music so loud?" she asks.

By the fourth inning, Emma is ready to leave. "I get it. They hit the ball and run around the bases."

Josh chuckles. "There's a little more to it than that."

Emma checks her phone. "That new Matthew McConaughey movie is playing in forty minutes. If we leave now, we could make it."

"I don't want to see the new Matthew McConaughey movie. I want to watch the rest of the game."

Emma's face gathers into a mild pout. "But I'm *bored*."

As soon as he and Emma part at the train station, Josh calls me. "She doesn't have to like baseball. She doesn't even have to *pretend* to like baseball. But she could have at least attempted to be interested—or at least be willing to sit through the game, because she knew I liked it. But, apparently, Matthew McConaughey wins."

I laugh. "Well, you've hit five dates. Do you have a verdict?"

"Emma is smart, and very, very beautiful," Josh says wistfully. "But she will always put herself first. I think . . . she is not a high-quality human."

"You *think*?"

"No, I know. I'm just disappointed."

"Totally fair," I identify. "It's disappointing when it doesn't work out, especially when hopes are high in the beginning."

"Mine were, for sure. I took one look at her, and I was sure this was it. Then I got to know her . . . and now I'm sure it's not."

"One hundred percent sure? Because if there's even a sliver of a doubt, I'm going to make you go out with her again . . ."

"Yes, Aleeza," Josh says. "I'd even say 110 percent."

"Congratulations!"

Josh laughs. "I'll tell you something, though. If I had dated her my way, I probably would have ignored the signs for a lot longer. In some ways, it's easier to get swept up in the fantasy and pretend the trouble isn't there. It postpones the disappointment. But your way, I saw everything clearly right in the beginning. It made it impossible to ignore."

"Josh, are you saying you would actually consider doing it my way again?"

"You know," he says, "I just might."

Josh's story is proof that once you start looking for a high-quality human, it becomes obvious pretty quickly when you haven't found one. I'm proud of him for bypassing his old habits and not mistaking physical attraction for a healthy relationship. Did you notice how quickly his attraction to Emma faded once he began paying attention to her character? I'm thrilled that he was willing to hold off on too much physical contact, because it saved him unnecessary confusion. In fact, his self-awareness around using physical contact in an unhealthy way—*and then not doing it*—was, in my mind, a huge breakthrough.

While things didn't work out with Emma, I believe that this experience was a great kick-start on Josh's own high-quality human journey. His eyes are open, he's paying attention, and he's starting to see the importance that good character plays in a long-term relationship. So while he continues looking for his high-quality human, I have no doubt that he's going to do his best to become one himself.

## CHAPTER TWO TIP

Twenty Questions can be a great way to kick-start a conversation and help you and your partner get to know each other in a fun, low-pressure way. By including different types of questions, you can showcase different aspects of your personality. Just be sure not to ask them all at once! Sprinkle in some questions naturally during your date—you don't want to sound like you're conducting an interview.

### SERIOUS

1. What accomplishments are you most proud of?
2. Who are your role models?
3. If you could move anywhere and still have a liveable wage, where would you go?
4. What are a few things on your bucket list? Which one do you plan to do soonest?
5. If you could go back and win any argument with anyone, which one would it be?
6. If you could instantly have any talent or skill, which would you want?
7. What did your grandparents do for a living?
8. How does your current morning routine compare to your ideal morning routine?

### FUN

9. What's a weird thing that stresses you out more than it should?
10. What did you get in trouble for in school?
11. If you don't like a book or movie, at what point would you stop?

12. In what order do you assemble your s'more?

13. What was the last costume you wore?

14. True or false: it always tastes better with cheese.

15. What's your favorite Netflix show? (Correct answer: *Jewish Matchmaking* starring Aleeza Ben Shalom!)

## DEEP

16. What do you think happens after you die?

17. How many countries have you been to?

18. What have you dreamt of doing that you probably won't do?

19. What is your guilty pleasure?

20. What wouldn't you do for $500?

# CHAPTER THREE

# You Can Only Move as Fast as the Slowest Person

Benjamin is as solid as solid gets. While other kids spent their summers at camp or hanging out with friends, he was training to umpire Little League games, which paid him forty dollars a pop. It wasn't so that he could spend it on candy or video games; Benjamin used the money to pay back his parents, who had helped him invest in a vending machine. He got permission to place it on the campus of his high school, and by the time he graduated, he was able to pay for college himself. At twenty-nine, he's the owner of a small corporate research firm, and his days are as regimented as those on a Navy ship: wake up, feed the cat, CrossFit, work, thirty minutes of Duolingo (he's learning Spanish), then various evening activities. He has dinner with his parents every other Friday. He pays his mortgage on the fifteenth of the month. In his office, he has a large whiteboard calendar marked up with dates, times, and deadlines, so that everyone is working on the same timeline. He would seem uptight, maybe even compulsive, if it wasn't for his sense of humor about it. There is no one quicker to laugh at Benjamin's Swiss-clock brain than Benjamin.

The only thing off schedule for him is his love life, which he feels got a late start. True, he's been dating since he was a teenager, but none of his relationships have been too serious. "I take responsibility for that," he admits. "I've been hyper-focused on getting myself established. I never gave the women I dated enough attention."

Things changed two years ago when Benjamin's father died. "I had this moment when I realized that my work is important, but family is even more important. So I decided to start dating to find someone I could see myself building a family with."

Though Benjamin is a real catch—financially successful, solid, stable, marriage-minded, and handsome—finding his person has not been as easy as he thought. "It seems like I'm on a different schedule than people in my age bracket," he explains. "I'm focused on moving forward, while they want to just enjoy the present. I have nothing against that, but it's not where I am. There's a difference between people who have really been through something, like losing a parent, and people who haven't. You just don't look at things the same way. Typically, on the timeline of life, the serious things don't happen until after you're out of your twenties. It happened to me early. So I'm looking for something different than a lot of people my age."

It was for this reason that I decided to set him up with Lily. She's thirty-one and a PhD candidate in Molecular Biology at UCLA. Her life, like Benjamin's, is full and busy; alongside writing her thesis, teaching, and advising students, Lily leads a "Compulsive Gardeners" club at the Los Angeles County Arboretum (of which Lily's dog, Matilda, is the unofficial mascot), and is a daily swimmer. A self-proclaimed "science geek," Lily has always been obsessed with the inner workings of the world around her (example: her childhood best friend was a flower). In eighth grade, she won a scholarship to spend the summer studying dolphins in Hawaii, and in college she did an apprenticeship in Barbados, studying the benefits of sea moss. Lily has an astounding knowledge of the natural world and her enthusiasm about it is infectious; even unscience-y folk like me can't help but be fascinated when she talks about it. It's no wonder that Lily's students absolutely adore her.

Lily has a maturity I knew Benjamin would appreciate. She's warm, personable, highly intelligent, and has one of the loveliest smiles I've ever seen. She, too, has been looking for someone future- and family-focused. Lily thought she had found it with her former fiancé, Evan, whom she dated for four years before he broke off their engagement and left her for a friend of hers. It's been a year since then, and Lily reached out to me for support as she dipped her toes back into the dating pool.

This was one of those opportunities I treasure, to set up two clients and advise them both as they go. Rarely have I ever seen sparks fly like this; when Benjamin and Lily met, it was like July 4th, Cinco de Mayo, and Chinese New Year all rolled into one. It's always nice to be right, but in this case, I was *darn* right.

It's been almost four months since Lily and Benjamin have started dating, and I've had the pleasure of watching it unfold up close. Benjamin loves Lily's depth, intelligence, and passion; Lily adores Benjamin's solidity, focus, and consideration for others. They laugh together a lot. And, so they tell me, the chemistry is through the roof. Benjamin already senses that Lily is his person, so he decides it's time to move things forward.

"My lease is ending in a few months," he tells her one Sunday afternoon as they lounge on his couch. "I'm debating whether or not to renew."

"Why not?" she asks. "This place is great."

"True, but space-wise, it really only works for one person. Not so ideal in the long-term."

Lily, always quick, gets his gist. "How long-term are you thinking?"

He smiles at her. "Pretty long."

To his surprise, Lily's face goes blank (he thinks?). In a flash, she's off the sofa and in the kitchen.

"You okay?" he asks.

"Yeah, just wanted a cup of tea. Do you have any more of that chai I like?"

By the time he unearths a rogue teabag from the back of his cupboard, the moment has passed. But Benjamin isn't giving up. A week later, during a discussion of their favorite holiday foods, he says, "My mom makes these latkes with leek and spinach that are so good, I dream about them sometimes. And I don't even like spinach."

"Sounds amazing," says Lily.

He grabs his moment. "When you come home with me this year, you'll try them."

There's that blank look again . . . but an instant later, Lily says, "Oh, my gosh! I saw this hilarious llama video yesterday—I can't believe I forgot to show you!" Just like that, her phone is out and she's pressing play. By the time the video is finished (she's right, it is hilarious), the subject of latkes has evaporated into the ether.

Benjamin decides to take the direct approach. It's the best way to determine if Lily's past reactions were only in his head, while making it clear to her exactly what he's thinking. On their four-month anniversary, he books a reservation at her favorite Indian restaurant and lays it all out on the table (alongside the naan and papadums). "I'm crazy about you," he says. "I know it hasn't been that long, but I think I'm ready to take things to the next level."

Lily's eyes shoot around the room, reminding Benjamin of a trapped animal. He was right; she's been avoiding the topic. But this time, she can't. Finding no way out, Lily takes a sip of water.

"Do you have a response to that?" Benjamin asks.

Her voice is quiet. "I don't know what to say."

"Say anything! Say, 'Sounds great, Benjamin. Let's talk about it' or 'Can I try your Baingan Bharta?' Just stop ignoring me every time I try to bring up our relationship."

"I just don't see why we have to make a whole big conversation out of it," says Lily. "Can't we just enjoy the moment and see how it goes?"

"I am enjoying the moment, but I'm also thinking about the future. You have to actually talk about the future if you want to have one together."

"I'm not ready yet."

"That's pretty obvious," says Benjamin, pressing his fork onto the table.

"What, you're mad now?" Lily exclaims. "You can't try to bulldoze me into a conversation that I don't want to have and then get mad at me for not wanting to have it!"

"*Why* don't you want to have it?"

"Why are you pressuring me?" Lily's response is louder than she intended, earning the glances of nearby diners. Lowering her voice, she continues, "I'm just not ready to think so far ahead."

"So, I'm just supposed to wait around until you are?"

Lily's eyes narrow. "Who's asking you to wait? If you're in such a big hurry, you're welcome to move on."

"Whoa, whoa, whoa," Benjamin says. "I don't want to move on. I want *you*. That's all I'm trying to tell you. I could see myself spending the rest of my life with you. I just want the rest of my life to start sooner than later."

"That's very nice, but it's not just the rest of *your* life we're talking about here. I have a life, too! A degree I'm in the middle of! A career I'm building! Just because you've decided it's time doesn't mean I have."

Benjamin rakes a hand through his hair. This is *so* not how he saw this evening going. "Lily, do you want to be with me?"

"Yes," she says, "but not if it means being forced to commit to something before I'm ready."

The evening ends in a tense stalemate. As soon as Benjamin drops Lily at her house, he picks up the phone and calls me.

"Okay, let's relax for a minute," I say after Benjamin tells me about their date-gone-wrong. "Let's take some perspective here."

"Perspective?" Benjamin says. "I try to tell her I want to spend my life with her and we end up in a fight!"

"A good fight," I say.

"Is there such a thing?"

You bet there is. In my world, there are two kinds of fights: good fights and bad fights. Bad fights are when two people actively try to hurt each other and tear each other down. They're destructive rather than constructive, separating rather than connecting. In good fights, two people are trying to build something, but just need some help communicating about the best way to do it.

"You two were both saying the same thing: 'I want to be with you,'" I say. "You were just saying it differently."

"I don't know," says Benjamin. "If Lily was so quick to write me off, maybe she doesn't feel as much for me as I do for her."

"That's impossible," I reply. "I've seen you together; the sparks between you two could cause a forest fire. My guess is that this isn't about your connection, but about speed."

In dating, as in life, you can only move as fast as the slowest person. Have you ever taken a walk with someone whose pace is slower than yours? You're really moving, but they're out of breath trying to keep up with you. If you want to walk together, the only solution is for you to slow down.

I suspect that the same thing is happening between Lily and Benjamin. He's in go-mode; he's found what he wants and sees no need to waste time. Lily is working toward the same finish line as Benjamin, but she's just taking it more slowly. (That's fine, but I'm curious to find out why.) In the meantime, if Benjamin wants to stay with Lily, he's going to have to meet her where she is or risk scaring her off.

"So, what, I just wait around until she decides she's ready?" Benjamin asks.

"Yes and no. You've been dating for four months, right?"

"Four months and five days," he says, a typical Benjamin reply.

"I want you to give this to the six-month mark. If it's working, then Lily is your person. If not, you cut bait and go fish in another pond."

This is true across the board, by the way. No matter what your background, if you're dating someone in a focused way, you should know by six months if this is your person. If you're feeling significantly confident, that's a yes. Significant doubt means it's a no. It doesn't mean you have to get married at six months. You don't even have to *propose* at six months. But at that point, it should be obvious whether you're in or out.

"So, basically, I'm being held hostage for the next two months?" Benjamin asks.

"That's one way to put it," I say with a laugh. "But if you really think Lily is your soulmate, I would try to look at it from another angle."

This is a lesson in patience, I explain, a skill that Benjamin's going to need if he wants to make any relationship work. This won't be the last time that he and his partner are out of sync, time-wise; there will always be someone ahead and someone behind, whether it be deciding on a wedding date, buying a house, or starting a family. In every case, *you can only move as fast as the slowest person.* "If you lack patience, it's not about Lily; it's about you," I say. "You may be able to keep everyone at your company on the same timeline, but it doesn't work that way in relationships. Good partners don't demand that things progress according to their schedule; they compromise to find a solution that works for everyone. So at this point, you have two options: you can be patient and wait for Lily and enjoy your time with her, or you could leave, which in my opinion, would be a waste."

"I agree," Benjamin cedes.

"Good. So relax. Give her her space. But make sure you gently nudge things along."

"How do I do that?"

"Think like water."

"Excuse me?"

In *The Art of War*, Sun Tzu gives some of the best dating advice I've ever heard: "Water shapes its course according to the nature of the ground over which it flows; the soldier works out his victory in relation to the foe whom he is facing."

In other words, you can't win a person by forcing your way in. You have to flow along their path at their pace.

"Let me talk to Lily," I say, "and then we'll strategize."

As soon as I hang up with Benjamin, I call Lily. She picks up on the first ring. "Let me guess," she says. "Benjamin called you."

Smart girl.

"Alright, Lily, spit it out. What's going on?"

I hear her sigh deeply. "He's amazing. I know that. And I'm so excited about us. But when I think about our future, I just freeze up."

"Why do you think that is?"

"Well, first of all, my life is crazy right now. My PhD program is so intense, I can barely see next week, let alone the rest of my life."

"How far along are you in the program?"

"About halfway. Two more years to go."

"Okay, so there's an end point. It won't always be like this."

"True, but if I get distracted, even by someone as awesome as Benjamin, it could take even longer."

"But I thought you were serious about meeting someone and moving ahead. Isn't that why we started working together? Didn't you ask me to set you up with someone marriage-minded?"

"Yes, you're right," she says, "but I guess I just didn't expect things to happen so quickly. I mean, I think Benjamin would get engaged today if I was open to it. Getting engaged and planning a wedding, that could throw off my entire program. I don't want to risk that. I've worked too hard to get where I am."

I hear this constantly. In the modern world, we're taught to get those degrees so we can lock down the job, buy the big house, the nice cars, and all the throw pillows from Home Goods and live happily ever after.

But how happy is ever after if you've got no one to share it with? My opinion—and I know it's an unpopular one—is that the most important thing for you to graduate with is your person. Here's why: too many times, I've seen people spend their twenties and thirties chasing the degrees and the careers, then wake up as the big 4-0 rolls around and realize they haven't found someone yet. They desperately jump into the dating market and are shocked at how hard it is to find someone of quality.

This is when they call me. "Why can't I find my person?" they wail.

"Well, you may have missed them," I say. "Maybe they were there when you were twenty-five, twenty-eight, thirty, but you weren't paying attention. So they found someone else."

The longer you wait, the harder it is to find everything you're looking for, I tell Lily.

"Benjamins don't come around every day. If you're lucky, you get two, maybe three shots in a lifetime. We don't always know when it's going to happen, so you need to be ready when it does."

By the way, if happiness is what you're going for—and we're *all* going for it—a vibrant career is only one (small) slice of the pie. As columnist David Brooks recently wrote in *The New York Times*, "If you have a great career and a crappy marriage you will be unhappy, but if you have a great marriage and a crappy career you will be happy." Science backs him up on this. University of Chicago economist Sam Peltzman found that marriage was "the most important differentiator" between happy and unhappy people. In his book *Get Married*, University of Virginia professor Brad Wilcox calls marriage "the top predictor I have run across of life satisfaction in America." He continues, "When it comes to predicting overall happiness, a good marriage is far more important than how much education you get, how much money you make, how often you have sex, and, yes, even how satisfied you are with your work."

"So you're saying I should ditch my degree and get married?" Lily asks.

"Heaven forbid! You just have to get your priorities straight. It's very simple: people come before a piece of paper. Of course you're going to finish your degree, but you're not going to sacrifice your person in order to get it."

"This is a tough one for me to get on board with," Lily replied. "What about women being financially independent and self-reliant and never compromising on their hopes and dreams?"

"I'm for all of that. How do you think I got here? But let's be real. While you're chasing your hopes and dreams, you'll still be online every night, swiping, trying to find someone to date.

Because you don't only want independence. You want a partner to spend your life with."

"Fair," she says.

"Listen," I continue. "There's nothing more stable than a stable relationship—especially with a stable guy like Benjamin! You might as well stick around. You may have to adjust your timeline a bit—though my guess is you probably won't, because you'll have a supportive partner. Just don't hold up this relationship."

(For the record, I would say this about any major life situation, be it a move or a job change or the sale of your business. These are all finite circumstances in what is, hopefully, a very long life. Have in mind that while all of these transitions are important, finding your person is the priority.)

"I'm with you," she says. "But I have to be honest. It's not just the degree thing that's blocking me. There's something else."

From the beginning of this conversation, I suspected there was something that Lily wasn't telling me. Over the years, my Spidey senses have become attuned to this sort of thing. People start out with a song and dance about their degree or their business or pressing family obligations, when really, there's something going on underneath that's blocking their dating and relationships. Lily's concerns about her career and women's empowerment are valid, but they're not her real issue. Now I'm excited, because we're going to get to the meat and potatoes.

"Tell me."

"I think . . . I still have some residual feelings from my breakup with Evan."

"What kind of feelings?"

"Being cheated on and left like that still hurts. Especially when I thought this was the person I was going to marry. The disappointment, you know? The *grief.* Not to mention the beating my self-confidence took . . ."

"This makes perfect sense. It's only been a year, Lily. It takes time to heal."

"I thought I was okay," she says. "I've done a lot of work to get through it. But now that it's getting more serious with Benjamin, these old feelings are coming up again . . ."

People often think this is a problem, but it's not. Every relationship we've ever been in leaves its imprint on us, for better or worse. It's unrealistic to think that we can simply erase our experience and move on with a clean slate. Ultimately, these relationships form us into who we are. It's natural that our memories of old relationships get stirred up by new ones. This only becomes a problem when we confuse our previous experience with the present one. Or, even more dangerous, when we romanticize our past partners and compare them with our present relationship; naturally, the new guy always comes up short (we'll talk more about this in Chapter Five). It doesn't sound like Lily is flying in that danger zone, but just to be safe, I ask, "So you don't ever see yourself getting back together with Evan?"

"Absolutely not," she says. "Looking back, it's obvious that he wasn't right for me at all. But I don't think I could take being abandoned like that again."

Lily is at a critical crossroads I've seen many times with many clients: she's found someone truly special, but if she doesn't let go of her old baggage, she won't allow herself to be fully open to a relationship with him. Instead, as he tries to get closer to her, she'll run farther and farther in the other direction.

We can't let that happen.

I launch Lily into a lightning-speed, abbreviated version of *Dating Detox*, a workshop I designed to help my clients shake off the residue of previous relationships, get a fresh perspective, cultivate new energy and focus, and get ready to find their soulmate. Typically, the people who take *Dating Detox* are single, burned out from the dating scene, or coming off a breakup. They may commit to two weeks, thirty days, or even three months to do this process. But as Lily is in a healthy relationship that we want to move forward, we're going to crunch it down into one conversation. Hopefully, we'll be able to start busting open Lily's baggage, taking out the excess, and getting her back on the road.

"You don't get graded on this," I say. "I'm just going to ask you some questions, and you answer them as honestly as you can, okay?"

"Okay."

"Is Evan the only partner who ever left you?" I ask.

"No. In all of my past relationships, they ended it."

This leads me to my next question: "Who started it?"

"Me," she says.

"So you're always the pursuer."

"For sure," she agrees. "If I want something, I go get it."

I like Lily's confidence to go after what she wants. It will serve her well in life. But in dating, it's not necessarily an asset. Here's another unpopular opinion: in every relationship, there's a pursuer and the pursued; in my world, the pursuer should be the man. Men, by nature, are providers. By winning and providing for the woman they choose, they feel secure and wanted. Women have this same need, but they meet it in the opposite way—by receiving. Receiving what a man provides makes a woman feel appreciated, loved, cared for, and safe. This feeds her appreciation for him, which boosts his confidence as a provider. With both of their fundamental needs met, so the relationship grows.

When a woman pursues, however, she might get her man, but her need for security will not be met in the same way. She might question herself: *Did he really want me, or did he just give in?* Those moments of insecurity can form cracks in her confidence, and the relationship. Many times, I've seen women in Lily's position sabotage or end relationships that have potential because they're never fully secure. Men in these relationships are often flattered in the beginning, but eventually, it undermines their confidence as providers. After all, what can they give to a woman who can go get it herself? In the end, these men often find a new receiver and pursue her (hence, Lily repeatedly getting dumped). It might be painful, but it's not personal. It's just human nature.

"Has anyone ever pursued you, Lily?" I ask.

"Only one person: Benjamin."

Bingo.

"Hmm," I say. "That must feel different."

She chuckles. "It's terrifying!"

"How come?"

"I've always been the one moving things forward. This is the complete opposite."

"Is that a bad thing?"

"Not exactly. I'm just . . ." She pauses for a minute and takes a shaky breath. "I'm scared he's going to figure out that I'm not worth the effort."

Her voice sounds like she's on the verge of tears.

"Do you think that's true?"

"Intellectually, I know I'm a good person," she says with a sniffle, "but after being left so many times . . . You can know something and not feel it."

"Jewish tradition says that the longest distance in the world is between the head and the heart," I say. "But that doesn't mean we can't bridge the gap. You've been the pursuer for your entire dating life. Now you have the chance to let someone else do the chasing."

"But now he's pushing me to move things along . . . I just don't want to lose control of my life."

"Is having control important to you?"

She laughs. "Hello? You've seen my apartment!"

That's true. The first time we met at Lily's, I noticed right away how everything is neatly arranged, the books on her shelves alphabetized, her pantry organized by color, with neatly written labels affixed to her kitchen cabinets. This is a woman for whom order and control are clearly a big deal.

This is actually one of the reasons I thought of Benjamin as a good match for her. They're both Type-A people; they'll be able to rely on each other to keep their lives in stable order. But with that comes the likelihood that they will irritate each other if both Lily and Benjamin insist on doing things *their* way. I suspect Lily senses this, especially now that Benjamin is talking about the future, and it's freaking her out.

"It's not easy to introduce another person into your life and still keep things status quo," I say. "Until now, you've made the rules. You've chosen who to date, you've gone after them, and you've fit them into your life the way you wanted. But with Benjamin, all the rules are changing. No wonder you're scared. But I encourage you to go with it anyway, even though it's uncomfortable, and see what happens. Maybe you'll get a different result than the one you've always gotten."

"Are you sure you're not a therapist?" Lily says.

"No, no, no, my friend. I do plenty of things, but therapy ain't one of them."

Knowing what we know now, Benjamin and I make a solid plan and timeline. For someone who loves schedules, this is right up his alley. Until the six-month mark, Benjamin is going to keep very tight boundaries around discussions of the past and future, sticking as much to the present as he can. If he does talk about the past, it should be about something that he and Lily recently experienced or a challenge they might have overcome together.

It's a great way to connect them and enforce the strength of their relationship.

Benjamin offers a perfect example: "We got lost trying to find our way out of Laurel Canyon. The Wi-Fi was awful and Waze wasn't working. At first, things got really tense, but then we talked through it and found our way out. By the end, we were laughing."

With the future, he has to tread lightly. If he wants to talk about upcoming plans, he needs to keep it within two months or less. Farther ahead will scare her off. "Ask her what she wants to do on Labor Day Weekend," I say, "not Thanksgiving."

This balance between past, present, and future will glue Lily and Benjamin together as a unit without pressure, but will help them move forward organically.

After apologies and an honest conversation, Benjamin and Lily move forward from their disaster date. The following week, Lily (and Matilda) take him for a drive along the Pacific Coast Highway and a hike at Point Dume. As they weave through sprays of coastal plants with the coastline beyond, Lily explains the name and derivation of each one. He wants to ask her if she's thought about having children—she has so much to teach them—but pockets the question for later. Instead, he just smiles.

"What?" she asks, smiling back.

"I was just thinking how no one else I know uses the words *leymus condensatus* in casual conversation."

"I'm impressed you remember it," she says.

"I remember everything you tell me. Even Matilda's full name."

"Prove it."

"Matilda Luna Lovegood Goldblum. After Jeff Goldblum."

She laughs. "I told you that, like, two months ago!"

"I know. And you said I would never remember it."

"Guess I was wrong."

"Don't worry," he says, slipping his hand into hers. "I won't tell anyone."

Two weeks later, he sees that the Red Hot Chili Peppers are playing in town on Halloween. He immediately wants to order tickets for himself and Lily but holds off, knowing it's beyond the two-month mark. He saves the link, though, so he can ask her in August.

Lily, meanwhile, is recognizing fear blocks when they come up and challenging herself to stay present. One of the things she likes most about Benjamin is how generous he is with compliments, but she can't stand the push-pull feeling that comes up in response, like she wants to run to him and run away from him at the same time. In the past, not knowing how to handle it, she's brushed his compliments away like lint off a sweater. Now, she pushes herself to smile and say, "Thank you. That makes me feel good." It feels vulnerable at first, but these small changes help her open herself to Benjamin—and her genuine feelings for him.

As their five-month anniversary approaches, Benjamin asks her what she wants to do. Instead of picking something, she hands him the reins: "Why don't you surprise me?" They go to a cat cafe to drink coffee and snuggle kittens looking for new homes.

"If I do end up getting a bigger place," Benjamin tells her, "there might be room for one of these guys."

"And Matilda, of course," Lily replies.

It takes everything in Benjamin's power not to fist-bump the sky.

By the time Lily and Benjamin hit the six-month mark, it's clear: they both have found their person.

Timing, however, is still an issue.

As before, Benjamin wants to get the train out of the station. But Lily is in no rush. He feels frustrated; she feels pressured. Oh, the irony: two people who love each other so much, but they can't figure out when to be together.

I've seen this many times, and it's caused the unfortunate death of many potentially beautiful relationships. Sometimes, the one who's forced to wait finally loses patience and gives up. Other times, the other one cracks under the pressure and leaves—or worse, gives in before they're really ready. I knew one woman who, after an ultimatum from the man she was dating, agreed to an engagement even though she wasn't ready. While they planned the wedding, her anxiety increased to the point where she had to be on medication. It wasn't that she didn't love this man, she just needed more time. However, the anxiety became so intense that she finally called off the wedding.

This is the story I tell Lily and Benjamin when they finally come to see me.

"Alright, guys," I say. "You clearly care deeply for each other. Dare I use the *l* word here?"

They look at each other and smile.

"You want to be together?"

"Yes."

"This person is your person?"

"Yes."

"Alright. So let's play a game."

I hand them both a piece of paper and a pencil and sit them at opposite ends of the table.

"This game is called DEW Date: Dating, Engagement, Wedding. I am going to ask you about each of these steps, and you are going to write down the date that feels right to you. Ready?"

They nod.

"When did you start dating? Write that down."

This one's easy. They're both done in seconds.

"When do you want to get engaged? Write it."

This time, as Benjamin scribbles away, Lily looks at her paper with a pensive expression, then back up at me, then down at the paper again. He's done well before she is.

"Now, ideally, when do you want to get married? Put it on paper."

Once again, Benjamin quickly has his answer down. Lily, on the other hand, starts writing, stops, erases what she's wrote, writes again, erases again, and finally, with a frustrated grunt, commits an answer to paper.

"Now, we're going to take a look at the dates you both wrote down and see how they line up. Expect them to be different. And no judgment, okay?"

"Okay."

Benjamin's paper is fairly predictable: They started dating in May. He wants to get engaged within the next month or two. And he envisions being married in eighteen months to two years.

Lily's answers surprise me: They started dating in May. She wants to get engaged in around eighteen months and married within the six months after that.

"Wait a minute," Benjamin says. "Our dates line up perfectly!"

"Well, sort of," says Lily. "You want to get engaged way earlier than I do."

"Yeah, but we want to be married around the same time!"

"That's true. I always felt like I wanted a quick engagement. No reason to waste time once you know you're really doing it."

"Benjamin, how do you feel about getting engaged so late in the game?" I ask.

"In my head I'm already engaged. It's kind of a long time to wait to make it official. And there's a part of me that wants to feel like Lily's in it with me."

"Lily, are you open to meeting Benjamin somewhere on the road?"

"Well," she says, "the reason I wanted to get engaged at eighteen months is that I'll have submitted my thesis by then. Then I'll have the bandwidth to plan a wedding. If we get engaged before that, it's going to be a huge stressor."

"We don't have to start planning right away," Benjamin says, tapping a finger rhythmically on the table. "We can always get engaged but hold off putting the wedding together until your thesis is done."

It's a sound argument, but Lily still hesitates. "Right, but you know my mom is going to want to throw a huge engagement party. That comes with its own set of commitments that are going to feel like a burden if I'm in the middle of a semester."

"Okay, how about this?" he counters. "We get engaged around eight, nine months from now—that's what, March?—on the provision that we hold off on all celebrations until the end of the semester."

Lily pulls out her phone and opens her calendar app. "I do have a few weeks open before I start teaching summer classes . . ."

"Perfect," Benjamin says. "You mom can throw the engagement party then. Then we can figure out a wedding date for after you finish your thesis."

"Does that work for you, Lily?" I ask.

"I think I'm okay with it."

"Great. So engagement in nine months and wedding around the eighteen- or nineteen-month mark?"

"I'm in," says Benjamin. "That was a lot easier than I thought."

But I can see that Lily is still wrapping her brain around it.

"Let's not make any final decisions today," I offer. "Sleep on it for a week and then we'll pick up the discussion where we left off."

Sometimes, these conversations can't be resolved in one shot. It may take one or two more sessions to find the right compromise.

No matter how long it takes, Lily and Benjamin need to keep their eye on the end goal of being together and supporting each other if they want to make this work.

## Epilogue

One year later, I receive a picture of Lily and Benjamin, smiling brightly in front of the ocean. She holds her ring finger, which has both a diamond and a wedding band on it, toward the camera. A message beneath says, *We eloped!*

I call Lily immediately. "Really?!?"

"Yes!" she exclaims. "The stress of planning everything was stopping me, but Benjamin needed to feel like I was really in. So I thought, *why not keep it simple and get married on our own?* We'll do an official thing after I'm done with my degree."

"That's amazing! Mazel Tov! Benjamin, how are you feeling?"

"Over the moon. Can you believe it was her idea?" he says with a laugh. "For the slower person, she moves pretty fast!"

## CHAPTER THREE TIP

## Aleeza's Relationship Growth Charts

My father once told me that in business, either you're going up or you're going down. The same applies to relationships. Of course, there are (brief) times when you can coast on cruise control, but ultimately, either you're trending up or the relationship is going down.

The graphs below give a clear picture of what I mean. Whether it's slow and steady, a windy roller coaster, or a crash-and-burn, the way your relationship progresses will tell you everything about its chances for survival.

### ESCALATOR

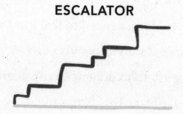

The sign of healthy progression is when there's a steady incline over time. This doesn't mean there won't be ups and downs; every relationship has them. But if, overall, you're moving upward, you're in good shape. (Word of caution: pay attention if things progress *too* quickly. In those cases, what goes up must come down.)

### FLATLINE

This is the graphical equivalent of *meh*. There's nothing wrong with this flatline progression, but there's nothing right, either. If you've put in adequate time and there's no incline, it's safe to say that this relationship is a code blue.

## LOOP-DE-LOOP

In a relationship like this one, you may experience some highs, but overall, you're retreading the same circle without getting anywhere. Even if it feels more exciting than a flatline relationship, you'll likely end up in the same place.

## CLIMB EVERY MOUNTAIN

When it's good, it's *so* good. When it's bad, it's torture. Sound familiar? Relationships like this one might be exciting and chock full o' drama, but it's completely unsustainable. In the end, it will combust and leave you absolutely exhausted.

# CHAPTER FOUR

# Overcoming Dating Anxiety

Anxiety has been Jonathan's companion since he was a kid. Firsts have always been tough for him: first days in a new class, first meetings with strangers, first dates. Even after years as a teacher, the first day of every school year has him contending with a loud inner dialogue of what-ifs and worst-case scenarios. This hasn't stopped him from finding success in life; Jonathan is kind, well-liked, and connected with his community. He's also found tools to help him, such as medication and weekly therapy. But it is a concerted effort for him to feel at ease throughout the day.

Jonathan's one outlet has always been music. From the minute he picked up a guitar when he was six years old, all the mental buzz went quiet and he could be fully present. When not in school, Jonathan spent hours practicing in his room. Once he'd taught himself every song in his parents' music books, he started writing songs of his own. In high school, Jonathan formed a band with a few friends called The Latchkee Kids and they earned a small following. Jonathan dreamed of being a rock star, traveling the world and performing for arenas full of screaming fans. A few years later, The Latchkee Kids had a minor hit that sent them on tour across the US, Japan, and Australia. Jonathan learned quickly that life on the road wasn't for him. The lack of routine and privacy and the wear of travel sent his anxiety skyrocketing. The runaway train of thoughts was so intense, he could barely concentrate offstage, let alone on it. The music that had helped him for years didn't work when he took it on the road. He decided that the price of this dream was too high; his mental health had to come first. When the hype of their single fizzled out, Jonathan bid goodbye to the band with no regrets and moved home to the Bay Area, where he grew up, and took a job as a music teacher with the San Francisco Public Schools. Ten years later, he spends his time teaching classes, directing a high school marching band, and giving private lessons. He still plays small, low-pressure venues around the city for local fans and friends. Admirably, he's built a life for himself that supports his mental health, meets his needs, and makes him happy.

"Now I'm ready to find someone to share it with," he says.

It hasn't been easy for Jonathan to find a partner. Like going on tour, dating is a minefield of anxiety for him, making it difficult for Jonathan to get the clarity he needs to make decisions about his relationships. Exhibit A: his last girlfriend, Annabel.

"We started dating two years ago," he says. "It was fine. She was really great. We had fun together—at least, I tried to have fun when I wasn't completely in my head about the whole thing. All I could think about was how I felt, how she felt, if we could actually make it work, how soon it would all fall apart."

"Why did you assume it would fall apart?" I ask.

"My parents had a horrible marriage, got divorced, and then remarried multiple times. It was a disaster," he replies. "So I assume that every relationship is a ticking time bomb that will eventually explode."

After eight months, Annabel told Jonathan that she wanted to get more serious, but sensed that he wasn't fully invested. "She was right. My anxiety was holding me back from really giving it a shot. But I didn't know how to *not* do that." Try as he might, he couldn't get out of the tangle of thoughts to discern what he wanted. The intensity was too much and he broke things off. "I felt horrible afterward. I don't think Annabel was the one, but I couldn't even stick around to find out. This isn't the first time I've done this, by the way. Every time things start moving forward, my anxiety just gets the best of me—even when I know better! I feel like one of those screaming toddlers on the first day of preschool; you can tell them that everything's okay but they can't hear it."

"Ironic," I reply, "because they're usually so happy once they get in the classroom."

"I want to be able to have a real relationship, but I keep getting in my way. What do I do?"

This is a story I've heard many times. Anxiety is a very real mental health issue for people like Jonathan, but even those without a clinical diagnosis have anxiety when it comes to dating. This is why I developed an approach like date 'em 'til you hate 'em, to take away all the mental chatter that can get in the way of real clarity. However, in cases like Jonathan's, a simple mindset might not be enough.

From my experience, anxious people live in their heads and not on the date. They are constantly evaluating: *Do I like this person? What if they don't like me back? Will this work out? What if something happens in three years?* Their minds are either in the past—in Jonathan's case, his parents' failed marriages—or in the unknown future, which they try to control by asking themselves questions and then answering them. This inability to live in the present makes anxious people consistently uncomfortable and feeds their anxiety. They don't know how they feel in the moment because they're never *in the moment.*

You might assume that as their concerns are resolved, the anxiety will dissipate. For example, let's say that Jonathan is worried that a date's strict veganism will prohibit them from being able to go out to eat together. But then he sees plenty of great dining options around the city. Problem solved, right? Wrong. When a person lives with anxiety, it's not about the issue that's bothering them; it's about the constant, high-frequency nervous energy that they need to direct at something. It's hard to believe, but finding a problem to be anxious about is a coping mechanism to manage that energy. So even after the restaurant issue is resolved, Jonathan will find something else to worry about, like a dog with a bone. His brain will always come up with a problem *because he needs one.* He might worry about finding parking or the restaurant double-booking their table. It's just how his brain works.

It's obvious that making decisions can be difficult for anxious people—especially when it comes to dating. It's not easy to get clear on the present moment when you're reliving the past or obsessively predicting the future. Many times, they make decisions based on past experiences or faulty predictions instead of the simple reality in front of them. While people without anxiety might choose to take time with decisions, anxious people often pressure themselves to choose *right now* because they're afraid of messing things up or missing an opportunity that may never come again. On the flip side, they might pummel themselves with so many doomsday predictions that they become incapable of making *any* decisions. In fact, they may break off the entire relationship just to escape the ordeal.

I have a lot of empathy for Jonathan's situation. It's hard enough to date without anxiety, let alone with it. But it's certainly not impossible. I've worked with plenty of anxious people who have found great partners and have built happy relationships with them. There's no reason why Jonathan can't, too.

Instead of a simple mindset, we're going to arm Jonathan with some tools to help him focus, keep calm, and stay clear. The first one is *practicing presence.*

"Are you dating anyone right now?" I ask.

"I'm supposed to go out with this woman, Maya, that a colleague set me up with. I haven't met her yet, but she's supposed to be great."

"Perfect. So you have a clean slate. No past experiences, no major expectations. The trick is to keep your head away from the past and future and focused on the now. The easiest way to do that is to make the date about Maya. Ask her about herself. When she talks, you listen. Let what she says lead to your next question. Think of it like breadcrumbs in the forest: just follow."

"But what happens if I start to tailspin?"

"You're going to pay attention to something in that moment—maybe it's Maya's earrings or the color of the tablecloth or the taste of your dinner—and you're going to make that part of the conversation."

I give Jonathan two other simple, straightforward tools to help him "bookend" each date. Before he goes out with Maya, he's going to *journal* or list his thoughts and worries so that they're on the page instead of taking up real estate in his head. If he wants, he can throw it out, rip it up, or burn it. If he typed it, he can email it to me. These ritual gestures are a way for Jonathan to "let go" of those thoughts so he can move forward with clarity.

After the date, he's going to call me (or another trusted, objective person) to *process* what happened. This will help Jonathan keep perspective, talk through any challenges that may have come up, and develop a game plan for the next date.

"Sometimes, your mind can feel like a maze," I say. "It's easier to find your way out when there's someone with you."

"I like that," Jonathan replies. "Let's give it a shot."

## Date One

Maya does not like Mexican restaurants. This might be surprising, considering that her mother, who hails from Mexico City, raised her on a steady diet of *tamales, chiles rellenos,* and *chilaquiles.* But that's precisely the problem: her mother's magical cooking trounces any other Mexican fare, no matter how "genuine." For Maya, going out to eat at a Mexican restaurant is an exercise in disappointment.

But, this time, she doesn't mind so much because she's at a Mexican restaurant with Jonathan.

When her friend Melissa, who knew Jonathan's colleague, said she had a great guy for her, Maya had rolled her eyes. She's been on enough bad dates that, at this point, it's more appealing for her to curl up with her cat, some Triple Caramel Chunk, and *Bridgerton.* But when Melissa begged her, she couldn't say no.

"I promise you, he's amazing!" Melissa insisted. "You're going to call and thank me after."

Maya sighed. "If this date sucks, you owe me a pint of Ben and Jerry's."

The odds of that were looking good when Jonathan recommended they meet at Padre Luis, a new place that everyone was raving about but Maya assumed would be lackluster. But she's surprised by both; the restaurant is half-decent and Jonathan is easy to talk to. He's also much better looking than she expected.

Jonathan, meanwhile, is wowed by Maya, who's lovely, funny, and fascinating. "I only ever think of music as an auditory experience," he says. "It's crazy how you can bring it to life for people who can't hear it."

"It's actually not that hard," she says. "I've been doing it for my brother, who was born deaf, since we were kids. You learn the lyrics and then you sort of act it out while you sign. It's like a play. And a lot of the time, deaf people can feel the bass and drums, so they get a sense of the rhythm."

"That is so cool."

"Yeah, that's how I know the lyrics to almost every song that came out since, like, 1999." Suddenly, her eyes widen. "WAIT! *That's* how I know you! You're Latchkee Kids!"

Jonathan covers his eyes. "That's me."

"No way!" Maya starts to sing. "*Got my sweater and my shoes, got an open hour or two, all I'm missing now is you . . .*"

"That's pretty good!"

"Yeah, right. There's a reason I'm a sign language interpreter and not a singer."

Jonathan is thrilled by their easy rapport . . . but the minute he realizes it, that familiar ball of anxiety forms in his throat. Thoughts start coming at him like machine gun fire:

*I like her . . . but how do I know?*

*Maybe it's just physical. She's beautiful.*

*Does she know I think she's beautiful?*

*Is that creepy?*

*Maybe I just like that she likes music. We might be completely incompatible.*

*Does she like me?*

*Is she really as great as she seems?*

*Does this have any potential?*

*Do I want it to have potential?*

*I think so, but it's only the first date . . .*

He feels his mind taking over. While he doesn't need to bolt from the restaurant—he's enjoying himself too much for that—it's not easy to swallow his *tacos al pastor*. He notices an inner part of himself take a step backward, disengaging from the conversation and becoming a spectator rather than a participant.

"You want some more water?" Maya asks. "You just got a little pale."

"I'm okay. It's just been a long day."

"Maybe we should cut it short so you can get some rest?"

"No, no," he says. "I'm really enjoying hanging out with you."

Maya smiles.

Jonathan takes a deep breath and remembers my advice to stay in the moment. He runs his hand nervously along the seat cushion, feeling the rough fabric under his fingers. "I like the pattern on these seats," he says, feeling ridiculous but doing it anyway.

"It's called *Otomi*," Maya responds. "It's a special kind of Mexican embroidery. My *abuela* does it. She makes these tablecloths that sell for hundreds of dollars."

"Really? Did she teach you how?"

"She tried, but I was hopeless . . ."

And just like that, the conversation is back on track again.

## Date Four

Surprisingly for Jonathan, things are humming along nicely with Maya and he's even landed himself a fourth date. Over the past few dates, Jonathan has gotten into the habit of *journaling* and *processing* with me, and when he feels himself falling into anxiety, he reminds himself to *practice presence*. It's helped him really get to know Maya, whom he finds to be warm, kind, and funny. Maya likes Jonathan's sense of humor and gentleness.

Before their fourth date, I offer Jonathan a new tool to put in his arsenal. It's called *investment*, or, as I like to call it, "acting as if."

Part of Jonathan's problem is his fixation on the future of his relationships. In his mind, it's only a matter of time until the worst-case scenario happens. This affects the way he engages with his dates and, ultimately, causes him to hold back his emotions. His dates can't help but sense this, and Jonathan, unable to handle the push for deeper connection, pulls the plug. It's the ultimate self-sabotage; by acting as if the relationship will inevitably implode, Jonathan inadvertently causes the outcome he most fears.

This tells you a lot about the power of the mind to affect the future. I'm not talking about psychic powers or divination; what I mean is, we have the capacity to visualize something in a way that's so palpable, so visceral, that it causes us to react like it's our reality. Those reactions inform our choices, which *make* that visualization a reality. There's an old Yiddish expression that illustrates this idea perfectly: "Think good and it will be good." In other words, your thoughts can shape your life. This is an amazing power—as long as it's used for the good.

"Instead of handling this relationship like a ticking time bomb," I say, "we're going to assume that it's going to work out beautifully."

"But it might not," says Jonathan. "In fact, it probably won't."

"It definitely won't if you go into it that way. Of course there's a chance that Maya isn't your person. But if you act like she isn't, she won't be. We're going to flip the script to see if we can get a different outcome."

"I have no idea how to do that."

"Jonathan, you are an amazing visualizer and a deeply creative person. I want you to use this to your advantage. Close your eyes for a minute."

He looks at me in confusion, then complies.

"I want you to imagine that this relationship is already a done deal," I say. "The pressure's off; no matter what you do, this is going to work out. How does that feel?"

"Calm. Uncomplicated."

"Good! Now, knowing that this is true, how do you see yourself interacting with Maya?"

His eyebrows crinkle in contemplation. "Like . . . I can just enjoy being with her. Like I don't have to overthink it. I can just be myself."

Matchmaker Matchmaker

"*Exactly.* Now, on your next date, I want you to take this vision with you and act as if it's true."

Jonathan's eyes open. "But what if it isn't?"

"If it isn't, you'll find out eventually," I say. "But, in the meantime, give yourself a chance to be surprised."

Halfway into their date, Maya and Jonathan have already gotten lost four times.

"Are you sure we're going the right way?" Maya says, consulting the app on her phone.

"I don't think there's a wrong way," says Jonathan, "since we don't know where we're going."

Maya growls. "Why do they have to make these clues so crazy hard? It took us hours to break the first three. Didn't they say this scavenger hunt was family-friendly? If I can't figure it out, how's a kid supposed to?"

Jonathan reaches for the phone. "Let me see the clue again." He reads aloud: "'*skirt of water, cloak of stone, sorry goddesses wail and moan. As my cap reaches to the sky, a bride in my belly will vow and cry.*'" He looks up at her blankly.

"See?" Maya says. "Impossible!"

"Should we buy a hint?"

"For fifteen bucks? No way!" Maya says. "We're going to figure this out if it kills us."

"Death by scavenger hunt. I guess there are worse ways to go."

"We're sure it's not the bridge?"

92

"No goddesses on the Golden Gate that I know of," Jonathan says. "And anyway, when I typed it in they said it was wrong."

Maya flumps herself down on the short stone wall fronting an apartment building. "Now what?"

Jonathan feels himself begin to tense up.

*I was the one who suggested the scavenger hunt, and now it's backfired.*

*Did I ruin the date?*

*What if she never wants to see me again?*

Then he remembers our exercise and reminds himself, *No matter what, this is going to work out.* He takes a quiet breath then sits down next to her. "Why don't we call ourselves scavenger hunt failures and go get some dinner?"

"But that's such a waste!" Maya says. "Didn't you pay, like, forty dollars to sign us up?"

"It's just money."

She pulls back slightly. "What do you mean?"

"I mean, I'm not going to freak out about forty bucks."

"Who says I'm freaking out?"

"I didn't. All I'm saying is it's not a big deal to me."

"Well, that's nice," Maya says. "Not all of us have the luxury of money not being a big deal."

Jonathan is astounded by how quickly things have escalated. He feels his heartbeat speed up. "I . . . I didn't mean to offend you," he says. "What I meant to say was that the money doesn't feel like a waste to me because . . . because I got to spend that time with you."

"Oh," Maya says. "I'm sorry. I just . . . I grew up poor. Like, really poor. Money's one of those sensitive spots for me, you know?"

"I understand. I'm sorry."

"No, no, you didn't do anything wrong . . ."

They sit in awkward silence until Maya says, "Listen . . . I'm kind of tired from all that walking. I think I'm going to head home."

"Are you sure?"

"Yeah. I'll call you later, okay?"

Unable to think of anything to say that might keep her there, he replies, "Yeah, okay . . ."

And just like that, the date is over.


"I did everything you said," Jonathan tells me on the phone, "and I still ruined it!"

"You didn't ruin anything, Jonathan. You had a little blip. Blips happen."

"On the fourth date?"

"Sure. I know a couple who got into an argument on their first date, and they've been married for twenty years."

"I worked really hard to visualize this relationship going well and then it didn't."

"What do you mean? It's not over."

"She left in the middle!"

"That's okay. This is part of a relationship. Just because there's a small conflict doesn't mean everything is shot."

Jonathan sighs. "I've only ever seen couples fight and break up."

"Which is why you're assuming that it's done with Maya. I promise you, it's not. Don't let anxiety and doubt make you shut down; now is exactly when you need to keep communication open. I say, send her a text."

"No way. I need to give her space. She said she would call me, remember?"

"Maya probably feels just as vulnerable as you do. I think a text will reassure her that you're still in."

"She won't think I'm being pushy?"

"Keep it low pressure and she won't. If anything, she'll appreciate it."

"I'm going to trust you," Jonathan says warily, "but if I scare her off..."

"...then you'll know she's not for you."


After Jonathan hangs up with me, he stares at his phone for a few minutes before deciding on a message: *The Palace of Fine Arts!*

A minute later he gets a reply from Maya: *?*

*Skirt of water, cloak of stone,* he writes. *There are goddesses on top of the building. "Brides vow and cry"—people get married there!*

He waits with anticipation for the speech bubble from her end. Finally, it comes: *You're a genius! Too bad we couldn't figure it out then.*

*Nah,* he replies. *We got to walk aimlessly around the city together!*

Maya sends a smile emoji. *Thank you. I thought you wouldn't want to talk to me after I blew up at you. I was really embarrassed.*

*It's okay,* Jonathan types back. *We all have our sensitive spots.*

He begins to write more, hesitates, and then reminds himself, *Act like this is a done deal.*

*What are we doing on our next date?* he writes.

*I'm game for anything,* Maya replies. *Well, maybe not a scavenger hunt.*

## Date Fourteen

Jonathan and Maya have been dating for six weeks. Over that time, Jonathan still has his moments of anxiety, but he's also been using the tools of *practicing presence, investment, pre-date journaling,* and *post-date processing* to help him. Jonathan has also started a daily mindfulness practice that includes deep breathing, guided meditation, and 15-minute "zen walks" in which he doesn't listen to music or podcasts, but is simply present with his surroundings. "I'm 'that guy' now," he says with a laugh. "All I need are some Tibetan singing bowls and a yurt."

"If it's working for you, I'm all for it," I say with a laugh. "How are things going with Maya?"

"I really, really like her. Maybe more than that. We get each other, you know?"

"I'm so happy. Have you told her that?"

"Yeah, she knows. We talk about everything . . . well, almost."

"Almost . . . ?"

"I haven't told her about my anxiety. I didn't want to bring in the heavy stuff too early."

That was a smart move on Jonathan's part. I know many people who, in the excitement of a new connection, spill all their secrets into a bowl too small to hold it. Inevitably, there's a mess everywhere.

Listen, we all have "stuff," whether it be medical or psychological conditions, loss and grief, trauma, etc. It's part of being human and nothing to be ashamed of. But it's important to tread carefully when introducing it to a new relationship. My guideline for sharing your "stuff" depends on the couple, but in general, it has to be at a point that you like and trust the other person enough to share this important information, but not too head-over-heels that you're unable to make level-headed decisions (in my opinion, that's about six to eight weeks into dating). One man I know waited too long to tell his partner that he had a daughter from a previous marriage. By then, they were both completely head over heels for each other and neither could think rationally. The woman convinced herself she would be happy to make it work. They married, and within a few months the woman realized she had no interest in being a stepmother. Very quickly, the marriage fell apart.

Before you tell your partner anything, you need to check your motives: What do you want to accomplish by sharing this information? Is it to enable the person you care about to know you better? Or are you using vulnerability to create an intimacy that isn't there yet? If you are someone who doesn't usually share that information but feel the desire to do so with this specific person, it's a good indicator that you should. But while some vulnerability is healthy, you don't want to set yourself up to be hurt. Make sure that your connection is strong enough to hold some extra weight. If you still fear you might risk the relationship by telling them something so personal, it might not be time yet.

But in the case of Jonathan and Maya, I think it is.

"Do you want to tell her?" I ask.

"I think . . . I think I do."

"Okay. Whenever that happens, keep it as simple as possible. No apologies, no shame. Just tell her the facts and answer her questions as honestly as you can."

"But what if she doesn't . . . ?"

"Jonathan, do you know what FEAR stands for?"

"I didn't know it stood for anything."

"Well, I like to say it's False Evidence Appearing Real. Fear tells us a story that's so realistic, so detailed, that we believe it. Right now, the story is that Maya is going to break up with you if you tell her you have clinical anxiety."

"Accurate."

"Now let's look at the facts. You and Maya have been dating for six weeks. You like her—maybe more than like her—and as far as you can see, she likes you back. You say you 'get each other' and you 'talk about everything.' If that's true, do you really think Maya is going to bail?"

"No, I guess not."

"Fear is just a trickster; don't let it distract you from reality. Just keep your focus on the facts and you'll do fine."

Jonathan invites Maya to his apartment and cooks her dinner: coconut butternut squash soup with lemongrass and truffle ribeye steaks. After a couple of glasses of wine, he says he wants to talk to her about something.

"Uh-oh," she says. "You can't make me a meal like that and then break up with me. It will ruin steak forever."

Jonathan laughs. "I'm not breaking up with you. That's actually the very last thing I want to do. I care about you a lot, and there's something I want to share with you." He takes a deep breath. "I have clinical anxiety."

She's quiet for a minute, then says, "That's it?"

"Uh, yeah?"

"I thought you were going to tell me you did time for murder or you've been married six times. Clinical anxiety? That's, like, every person."

"Not exactly. Mine's a little more serious than just regular anxiety. I have to take medication and go to therapy."

"That's good. I know a lot of people in the deaf community who deal with that. Not all of them are willing to get help. I'm happy for you."

"Did you just say you're happy for me?"

"Jonathan, everybody's got a thing. Yours is anxiety, mine is the fallout from growing up poor. I hoard stuff, I don't throw out anything, and I stock up on canned goods like the apocalypse is coming. I'm terrified of spending money, even though I have more than enough. It's a pain sometimes, but it's my thing. Now I know your thing."

"I just . . . I can't believe it."

"What, did you think I was going to break up with you?"

He blushes. "Maybe."

Maya leans over and kisses him. "Buddy, it's going to take a lot more than that."

## Date Twenty

A few hours before they're scheduled to meet at Pier 39, Maya gets a call from Jonathan. "I can't make it tonight. I'm not feeling well."

"Sick?" Maya replies. "Or anxious?"

She hears him sigh. "Anxious. I have days like this once or twice a year. It's bad. I can't really function so well."

"How about I come to you?" she offers. "We could watch *Brooklyn Nine-Nine* and get pizza."

"I think I just need to be alone."

His voice sounds small and sad. Her heart goes out to him.

"I'm sorry, Maya."

"Don't be sorry. I get it. You do what you need to take care of yourself."

"I wanted to push through, but I just can't. I hate that I have to be like this. I hate that you have to deal with this."

"Listen to me," Maya says. "I'm not dealing with anything, okay? This is part of who you are, and I want you. When someone loses their hearing, the hardest part isn't being deaf, it's when they don't accept that they won't hear again. I've seen people fight their deafness and refuse to learn skills that can help them. It's like running into a wall; it makes everything so much more painful. Don't make it worse for yourself by fighting. Just accept that you have anxiety and that you're having a bad day. I'm here for you no matter what."

"Thank you, Maya," says Jonathan. She thinks she hears his voice break.

"And when you're feeling better," she says, "I'm going to beat you at Skee-Ball."

## Date Thirty

*Excerpt from Jonathan's journal:*

*Today's the day. I've decided. I'm going to break up with Maya.*

*Aleeza says she thinks it would be a big mistake. "Hold on a second. Didn't you tell me that she's incredible and supportive and you're mad about her?"*

*It's true, I did. And I still think so. I've never met anyone like Maya. I've never felt so comfortable with another person. She's my friend and my girlfriend. But it feels too good to be true.*

*Of course, now I'm thinking of what Aleeza would say: "Think good and it will be good." I have to give her credit; so far, I've done that and it's worked. But how long can the magic really last? Eventually things are going to have to fall apart, right?*

*Then again, if Maya and I have made it this far—five months already—who's to say we can't keep it going?*

*Me, I guess.*

*So far, all the evidence has been pointing to this being a good thing. From the first date, it felt good with Maya and it only keeps feeling better. Just as important, I keep feeling better. I have to admit that since doing these extra practices that Aleeza recommended, and also my own, I feel more equipped to handle challenges. I don't kid myself that the anxiety will ever go away; we are together for life. But somehow, I'm not so afraid of it anymore. I don't feel like it's holding me back the same way. True, I have my bad days, and things set me off that most other people would walk through without a second thought. But it doesn't rule me the way it used to. I have the power to make choices; it doesn't choose for me anymore.*

*I just realized, as I'm writing this, that if I break up with Maya, who I adore, I would be letting anxiety choose for me. If it was up to me alone, I would spend every day of the rest of my life with her. So why would I not?*

*Okay, so maybe I won't break up with her.*

*I'll take her to the movies instead.*

## CHAPTER FOUR TIP

### Aleeza's Anxiety Meter

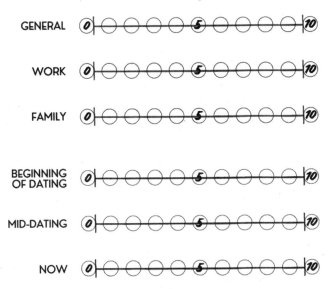

GENERAL

WORK

FAMILY

BEGINNING
OF DATING

MID-DATING

NOW

Dating anxiety can be difficult to navigate, but this tool helps you get some perspective. First, rate your general anxiety on a day off, when you have no work or family obligations. Next, rate your anxiety level at work, then around family. These measurements will serve as your baseline.

Now, rate your anxiety on your first date, your second, the middle of the dating period, and, finally, today. How does it compare to the overall anxiety you measured in the beginning? Has your anxiety level decreased or increased as the relationship has progressed?

# CHAPTER FIVE

# Rejection Is God's Protection

Amy and Charlie met during their freshman year at Northwestern University. Amy, a Chicago native, was a bubbly, friendly biology major with hopes of going into a healing profession (she wasn't sure which one yet, but she knew it would involve developing real relationships with her clients). Charlie, who grew up outside the city, was gentle and soft-spoken with a head for numbers; he'd earned a full scholarship as an applied mathematics major. Though their personalities couldn't have been more different, their attraction was immediate and intense; within a few days they were inseparable, and within a few weeks, they were in love. For the next three years, Amy and Charlie's romance played like one of those romantic comedy montages: sweet, funny, heartwarming. Every moment they spent together felt like magic.

This, my friends, is a first love. There's nothing like it in the world. First loves are lovely, tender, and unforgettable, sprinkling you with stardust that sticks for the rest of your life. If you're lucky, you marry your first love. But even if you don't, you will always look back on that person in soft focus, with romantic lighting and a symphony in the background.

As Amy and Charlie's first love stretched on, it didn't occur to either of them to think much about the future. They were in college, after all, barely out of their teenage years. And it was delicious to simply be together. But as their junior year drew to a close, Amy began to set her sights on what would come next.

"Do you want to get married?" she asked him late one night as they studied for finals.

"To you?" he replied.

She laughed. "Who else?"

"Yeah, I want to marry you," he said. "But you know I don't want kids."

Amy did know. Charlie had told her about his horrific childhood, during which he'd been shuffled from one foster placement to the next and endured all kinds of abuse. Luckily, a high school math teacher had taken Charlie under his wing, encouraged him, and even let him sleep on his couch so that Charlie could keep his grades up and graduate. That teacher had written Charlie a glowing recommendation that helped him earn his scholarship. With the support of a social worker and later, a campus therapist, Charlie had made a good amount of peace with his past. But he had also decided he would never have children. The memories of his own childhood were simply too painful; a child wouldn't be a joy to him, but a trigger.

Amy, however, believed deep down that with time, Charlie would change his mind. They loved each other. Surely he'd want to make a family with her one day.

She folded up the conversation and placed it in the pocket of her mind, where it stayed for the whole of their senior year. By the following June, Amy could only envision the rest of her life with Charlie. She was his person, and he was hers.

So she was shocked when, just a week after graduation, Charlie ended it.

"You're not making any sense," Amy said. "You love me."

"I do," he replied. "More than you can imagine."

"Then why are you doing this?"

"Because I can't give you what you want."

"What are you talking about?" she cried. "I want you!"

"You want a family, Ames. You want kids."

"So?"

"I don't."

"Sure, not now. But you will . . ."

"No, I won't," he said. "I never will."

His voice was as sure and unwavering as rock. For the first time, the truth hit her: he was serious. He didn't want to have children. Not ever.

Not even with her.

Amy's face fell. "But I thought . . ."

"That I'd change my mind?"

She didn't have to reply.

"Oh, Ames," said Charlie, his voice breaking. "I'm so sorry."

"Don't be sorry. *Be* with me."

"I can't."

The pain was so sharp, she cast her eyes to the ground.

"Look at me. Amy."

"I can't."

"*Please*, Ames. Don't make this harder than it is."

She heard the pain in his voice and forced herself to look at him. Charlie's face was a mask of anguish. He leaned his forehead against hers.

"I love you," he said. "I never loved anyone until I met you. I never *had* anyone to love before I met you. You showed me how."

Amy cried harder. "Charlie . . ."

"I want you to have everything you want," he said. "That's why I'm letting you go."

Ten years later, Amy still lives in Chicago. Now she's a women's massage therapist with a thriving practice of regulars who come for her healing touch, uplifting company, and gentle advice. Her favorite clients are the caregivers of children with special needs and the pregnant mamas who come in for prenatal massages, then bring their new babies to visit her. "Mothers need mothering, too," Amy says.

A couple of times a year, Charlie will drop her a text or an encouraging comment on social media. His intentions are friendly, and Amy responds in kind. But it often takes a few days to recover from his messages, especially if she happens to be post-breakup or during a dating slump. Charlie even sneaks into her thoughts sometimes when she's dating someone else (including a few men I've set her up with), but she's managed to put those thoughts in their rightful place and focus on the man in front of her. But all that changes when she starts getting serious with Ian.

Ian is a consummate "doer." After spending the first ten years of his career in the nonprofit sector, he saw the value of creating a "mother ship," as he calls it, in which struggling NPOs could join forces and benefit from a larger pool of resources. Just a few years later, he's now the founder of Chicago's largest nonprofit incubator. *Chicago Magazine* tipped him as one of the "Top 35 under 35" in the city—though it took two weeks for Ian to hear about it; he was in Nepal at the time, working on an underground piping project to address water scarcity in the region.

Ian is soft, good-natured, and focused, and from almost the beginning, he's been smitten with Amy. Amy feels herself falling for him, too, but something's blocking her from completely giving herself over to it.

"I do like him a lot—more than a lot," she admits to me. "He really listens when I talk to him. He asks these incisive questions that make me feel like he wants to know and understand me. But there's a piece of me that isn't fully in."

"What do you think it is?"

"I have no idea—which is so frustrating! Ian is everything I want: caring, intelligent, ready to settle down. I'm attracted to him. We have fun together. What's wrong with me?"

The answer becomes clear on her thirty-third birthday, when Ian goes above and beyond to celebrate. Knowing how much Amy loves horses, he takes her to a ranch outside the city where they saddle up for a three-hour trail ride. Ian has never been riding before; in fact, this is the first time he's been this close to a horse. Which is why he had no idea—until now—that he is terrified of them.

"You are such a good sport," Amy says over and over. "I'm so sorry . . ."

"I'm keeping things exciting," replies Ian with a shaky voice, his knuckles white from gripping the reins. "Surprise! I have equinophobia!"

Amy is grateful to be able to laugh out loud. "If it's any consolation, you're doing really well."

"You look happy," he says, "so it's worth it."

When they get back to the city (Amy drives so Ian can regain his bearings), they head to Amy's favorite dive bar, where Ian has arranged for a large group of Amy's friends and clients, as well as her brother, Jake, and his wife to surprise her.

"Oh, my gosh, this is crazy!" Amy exclaims. "How did you get everyone here?"

"I may have had to go into your phone and send myself some of your contacts," he says. "Then I had everyone spread the word. I hope you don't mind."

She doesn't. In fact, she's elated that Ian knows her well enough to have realized she'd love to celebrate her birthday this way, and with these people—and impressed he made it happen.

Jake's wife, Jules, leans into their conversation. "He was really sweet about it. He was like, 'I swear, I'm not a stalker!'"

"I like this one," says Jake, raising a glass of beer to Ian. "He's a good dude."

Amy smiles at Ian. "No one's ever done anything like this for me before."

He smiles back. "I'm glad to be the first."

A warm, sweet feeling floods Amy's chest.

The party is a blast, with Amy's guests laughing and talking over pitchers of beer and games of darts. Ian feeds quarters into the vintage jukebox and spins Amy in his arms to "Wake Me Up Before You Go-Go." She can't remember having this much fun or laughing this much in years.

On a quick bathroom break, Amy reapplies her lipstick and takes a quick glance at her phone. She has a text:

*Hey, Ames. Happy 33. Hope it's the best year yet.*

It's from Charlie.

It hits her like a gut punch: the party happening in her honor just outside the door falls away and all she can feel is longing for Charlie, wishing he was there with her.

"Are you okay?" Ian says when she comes back to the bar. "You look . . . I don't know . . ."

"Shouldn't have had that last beer," she says. "I think I need to go home."

The next day, Amy calls me. "I figured out the problem: it's Charlie."

"Tell me about it."

"When we broke up, there was a part of me that didn't believe it was over. I *still* don't believe it's over. There's always this lingering thought that someday, things will work out between us."

This is classic first-love thinking. It's almost impossible to fully walk away from something so pure and wonderful—even if there's no chance it could ever be again, and even if 99 percent of the heart has moved on. There is still that 1 percent that refuses to say die. This isn't necessarily a negative thing, unless that first love gets in the way of a new one.

"Ian is really similar to Charlie—they have the same kind of gentleness and something about their smiles . . ." Amy says. "Anyway, I can't help but compare them. And Ian . . . he's great, but it doesn't feel the same."

Of course it doesn't. Nothing ever measures up to a first love. Even if Amy was head-over-heels for Ian, and even if they had an absolutely wonderful relationship, the experience will never be anything like the one she had with Charlie.

"With Charlie, you had a first love," I explain. "There's history there. But with Ian, you have young love. There's a lot of potential, but you haven't put in the time yet to see what you could be together. It's like comparing a mansion to blueprints."

"But if the mansion is beautiful, why would I want to build something new?"

"Maybe there's a hole in the foundation," I say. "Remind me, why did you and Charlie break up?"

"He didn't want children."

"That's the only reason?"

"That's it. He said he still loved me, that he would always love me, but he wanted me to have what I wanted."

"Sounds like a good guy."

Amy groans. "Don't make it worse, Aleeza!"

"Just because he's a good guy doesn't mean he's good for *you*. He was doing you a favor by letting you go."

"What kind of favor leaves you with a broken heart?"

It's hard, when someone turns you away (for whatever reason), not to take it personally. Many people assume it was because of a lack on their part. If only they'd been more interesting, compassionate, smart, unique, or sexy . . . If only they'd done this or that . . . But the truth is, getting turned down, rejected, or dumped is one of the best favors someone can do for you. They're making it clear that they're not right for you and are freeing you to find someone who is a better fit.

Put simply, rejection is God's protection.

"But what if he is the right fit?" Amy counters. "There must be a reason I'm still thinking about him. It's been ten years. Maybe things have changed."

"I guess there's only one way to find out. Why don't you call him and ask?"

Now, before you get mad at me for sending Amy into the line of fire and risking her relationship with Ian, allow me to explain.

When someone holds on to an ex, mentally, emotionally, or physically, it's because it serves them in some way. Maybe it's just the pleasure of reliving the time together. Maybe they're protecting themselves with a fantasy instead of being vulnerable with a flesh-and-blood person. Maybe they're keeping them as backup in case nothing else pans out (think Julia Roberts in *My Best Friend's Wedding*). Or, in some cases, it could very well be that the relationship isn't over yet.

Either way, if they are still on your mind and in your life, that means you've decided there's still potential.

And if you genuinely believe so, it's up to you to explore it. Why should a good guy like Ian be with Amy if her heart belongs to someone else? And why, if Charlie and Amy are so mad about each other, shouldn't they be together? Better for Amy to reconfirm that things haven't changed on Charlie's end so she doesn't have to always wonder. If it works out, excellent. And if it doesn't, she'll be able to lay the question to rest and focus on Ian with a heart that's 100 percent ready for this new love.

(To be clear, I only recommend getting closure like this when you haven't been in touch with the person for an extended period of time and are reaching out to them *for clarification purposes only*. If there are any other motives besides this one, I strongly advise staying away.)

Amy's situation reminds me of a couple I know who dated for a few months and really liked each other, but they just couldn't make it work. They broke it off and dated other people for the next ten years—but neither could find their person. Many times, they both thought longingly of each other. Eventually, they reconnected on social media and now they're married.

When most people hear this story, they say, "How romantic! After ten years they found each other again!"

I say, "They wasted ten years they could have enjoyed together."

I understand that timing can play a role in these situations. It's very possible that they weren't right for each other the first time around. Both of them might have needed some more life experience to refine them into a perfect match. But imagine if they'd done the hard work in the beginning and resolved the issues they thought were insurmountable. I'm happy they found each other in the end, but I would have been much happier if they'd sealed the deal ten years earlier.

So if Amy and Charlie are really meant to be—or if they *aren't*—she needs to know now.

The lights of the Mediterranean restaurant on Hubbard Street are warm and low; the moment Amy enters and asks for her reservation, she notices her voice has fallen to just above a whisper.

"The rest of your party is already here," says the host, gesturing to a table in the back corner.

And there he is. Exactly as she remembered. Maybe even better.

When Charlie sees her heading to the table, his face breaks into a smile. He jumps up to greet her. "Ames!" he says, pulling her in for a hug.

Amy's heart does a flip-flop; she takes a deep breath to steady herself.

"You look amazing," he says, pulling out her chair. "Really great."

"You, too," she says.

They stare at each other for a minute before Amy says, "So . . . tell me everything."

As their first course comes and goes, Charlie talks about his job as a forensic accountant, analyzing financial records for legal cases ("I spend a lot of time as a witness in court," he says). He's just bought an apartment in Lincoln Park, he says, which he shares with his two dogs, Neil and Joni, and he started woodworking in his free time ("It's a lot more math than you think."). Amy tells him about her practice and her clients, and catches him up on her parents and brother. Their rapport is warm and easy, like slipping back into a favorite pair of jeans.

"Are you dating anyone?" Amy asks.

"Here and there," he replies. "I had a couple of serious relationships, but they didn't stick."

"How come?"

"Same reason you and I didn't stick," he says.

Amy takes a sip of wine. "So you still don't . . . ?"

"No," he says. "I haven't changed my mind."

Her hopes are instantly crushed, like a paper cup in his hand. "Can I ask you something?"

"Of course. I assume that's why you asked me to dinner."

She smiles. He always did know how she ticked. "Is it worth the trade-off for you? You'd rather be alone?"

"I'd rather be *honest*. If I forced myself to have a child just to make you or anyone else happy, it would be a disservice. To you, to me, and most definitely to that kid."

"So if I said I didn't want kids anymore . . ." she begins.

"You'd be lying," he replies. "And you'd regret it. Just look at the way you light up when you talk about your prenatal clients and their babies. The way you talk about *mothers*. You were meant to be one. I knew it even back then."

She sits back in her chair, slumped slightly in defeat.

"You dating anyone?" he asks.

"Yeah. His name is Ian. He's a really good guy. Gentle, attentive. He reminds me of you, actually."

Charlie eyes her. "You love him?"

"Not yet," she says, "but I think I could . . . if I could just let you go."

Unexpected tears fill her eyes.

"Ames," he says, taking her hand. "I know how you feel. I'll always treasure what we had. But the price is just too high, for both of us."

"He's absolutely right," I tell Amy when we meet to debrief. "He's an honest man who's trying to do the right thing."

"But that means giving up on real love," she says, tears spilling down her cheeks. "It isn't fair."

"You're right. But life isn't fair. Life is life."

"But didn't someone say, 'All's fair in love and war'?"

"That was John Lyly. And he was dead wrong."

Amy's argument smacks of the romantic comedy formula in which the couple decides to spend the rest of their lives battling through insurmountable differences in order to live happily ever after. It's sweet at the moment, but it always makes me cringe, knowing how miserable their happily ever after is going to be.

One of my favorite romantic movies is one that doesn't end happily: *The Way We Were* starring Barbra Streisand and Robert Redford. It's one of the most real depictions of a relationship in which two people deeply love each other but (SPOILER ALERT) can't make it work together. Katie's a firebrand political liberal; Hubbell's a laid-back, apolitical Hollywood writer during the McCarthy era. He just wants to sit back and enjoy life; to her, life is about improving the world and everyone in it. They separate and come back together, unable to live together and unable to live without each other. Eventually, they call it quits for good. In the last scene of the movie, they run into each other on the street in New York City. The love is still there; you can feel it between them as Katie brushes Hubbell's hair across his forehead, the way she used to when they were married. But they both know it's not meant to be.

I'll admit it: even I cry when I watch this scene. I want to shake them both and say, "COME ON! YOU CAN MAKE THIS WORK!" But they can't. They have a fundamental difference in values that can't be overcome.

This is what Amy is facing now.

Even the most profound, perfect love doesn't stand a chance against a values conflict. I've seen this play out hundreds of times. It might be hardcore political issues, religious beliefs or other ideologies, family obligations, and, of course, the desire to have (or not have) children. These core value differences are like the dealer in a casino; you may have a great hand and even take a few rounds, but eventually, the house always wins.

Some value conflicts are negotiable, depending on the level to which they trigger each partner. Think of it like a mosquito bite versus a snake bite. A mosquito bite is annoying, but you can live with it; a snake bite can be lethal. If, for example, one partner feels strongly about bringing religion into the home while the other is anti-religion, it could be a deal-breaker if they can't find a compromise. It depends on how much each is willing to give. However, there are core value differences that aren't negotiable, such as having children. If one wants children and the other doesn't, no love in the world can overcome that.

No one wants to hear this. I don't even like saying it. But it's true.

The hardest thing about values conflicts is that everything else about the relationship can be wonderful. You might get along perfectly otherwise. How can only one thing stand in the way? But if it's fundamental to who you are, that one thing is everything.

"So that's it?" Amy asks. "I have to just give Charlie up forever?"

"No, you don't have to give him up. You can have him. You just can't have children. Are you okay with that?"

"I don't know," she says.

"Then find out. Take some time to think about it until you're clear."

"And then what do I do?"

"That depends on what the answer is. If it's a yes, then be honest with Ian and go live your life with Charlie. But if it's a no, then you need to say goodbye to Charlie for good."

This may sound harsh, but firmly shutting the door on an ex is one of the kindest things you can do for yourself. Any kind of relationship with your ex keeps you tethered to the past; by making it clear that you are moving on, you have turned your focus from the past to the future. If Amy decides she wants a different kind of relationship than the one Charlie's offering, she has to be willing to let him go completely—or else keep herself in limbo indefinitely.

"But don't you always say, 'date 'em 'til you hate 'em?'" Amy says. "I don't hate Charlie; I'll always love him—even if I marry someone else one day."

"You're right; love doesn't disappear just because you choose not to be with someone. But remember, this isn't about actually hating the other person; it's about dating them until you find a real deal-breaker. I think we can both agree that not having children is a pretty big one. In this case, instead of date 'em 'til you hate 'em, I would say, 'dump 'em even if you love 'em.'"

"So if he really isn't for me," Amy says, "I can never speak to him again? Not even as friends?" she says.

"In my opinion, you can't be friends with someone you've already dated and still love," I reply. "Your past will always be there, and at least one of you will still want something more. Be honest: do you really think you could be 'just friends' with Charlie?"

"Probably not," Amy admits.

"Right. Amy, this is about more than deciding if you can live without children; it's about facing the ghosts of your first love. Do you want to resurrect them or bury them for good?"

"How will I know for sure what I want?"

"Just be honest with yourself," I reply, "and the right answer will come."

Over the next week, Amy thinks about the time she had with Charlie all those years ago: how beautiful and magical it was, and how good it felt to be with him just recently. Surely their potential future would be the same. They could make an amazing life together, full of fun, laughter, travel, walks in the city with the dogs, endless conversation. She has no doubt she would be happy with him—but she would also live with longing for something deeply important to her. Could she withstand that for the rest of her life in order to be with her first love?

She holds it up against a future with Ian, whom she is still seeing.

"Do you want kids?" she asks him one night as they walk home from the Adler Planetarium.

He smiles. "Sure, but . . ."

Amy braces herself for the worst.

"... I really want to adopt."

She bursts into surprised laughter.

"What?" Ian says, laughing, too.

"That's just not what I expected you to say."

"I mean, I want to have biological kids, too. But I feel really strongly about adoption. My sister's adopted; my parents brought her home from Honduras when I was ten. It was amazing for all of us. It's something I'd really like to do myself."

She smiles at him. "That's lovely."

"You're lovely," he says, taking her hand. "I want you to know I'm crazy about you."

She opens her mouth to answer, but he stops her.

"You don't have to say anything back," Ian continues. "I said it because I mean it. I know you're not where I am yet, but I'm willing to wait as long as it takes."

The clash of emotion comes on strong in Amy; she wants to both kiss him and burst into tears. Instead, she squeezes his hand and keeps on walking.

A few days later, Amy gets a surprise guest at her massage studio. Her prenatal client, Maeve, comes with a baby in a sling on her chest.

"Oh, my goodness!" Amy cries. "I didn't know you had him!"

"He came early. He needed a little time in the NICU but he's doing great now."

"Wow," Amy says, rubbing Maeve's arm. "And you're okay?"

"I'm exhausted! But I'm starting to get up and about again. I saw we had an appointment today, so I thought I'd bring him to meet you. This is Noah." She leans forward so Amy can see the little bundle in the sling.

"Noah!" Amy exclaims. "He's gorgeous!"

He makes a tiny squawk and rustles against his mother.

"Mind if I take him out for a second?" Maeve asks.

"Not at all!" Amy says. "Come in, come in, sit down . . ."

As Maeve sits and pulls the baby from the sling, Amy melts at the dark red mop on his head. "Look at that hair!"

"I know! I told my husband that people pay hundreds of dollars for color like that." Maeve sniffs the baby's bottom. "This guy needs a change. Can you hold him for a second?"

"Of course," Amy says, gathering the baby into her arms. Holding him against her chest feels like sliding into a warm bath. Her muscles relax and a sweet tenderness floods in, making her sigh with pleasure.

"It's the best feeling in the world, right?" Maeve says.

In a split second, Amy considers the question. She's felt many wonderful things in her life: the ocean breeze on a hot day; her grandmother's warm, silky skin; her first love with Charlie. But if this was how good it felt to hold someone else's child, she could only imagine that holding her own would eclipse them all.

She smiles at Maeve. "It really is."

That night, Amy tosses and turns in her bed as images of Charlie and Ian play over and over in her head like a tumble dryer. In the wee hours of morning, sleep finally takes over and she falls into a dream.

A costume party is taking place in a huge room lit by thousands of candles. Crystal chandeliers hang from the ceilings. Velvet drapes adorn the walls. Lace-covered tables are laid with rich delicacies. The room is crowded with people, all wearing masks, and in the center of them is Amy, wearing an ornate satin gown straight out of Versailles. She is the belle of the ball; throughout the evening, every man in the room takes Amy for a turn across the marble dance floor. But she is constantly looking over her shoulders, waiting for someone in particular to appear.

Then he does. Even in a mask, she instantly recognizes his smile.

*Charlie*, she thinks with joy and relief as she slips into his arms. They dance in a fluid motion, their bodies moving in perfect sync with each other. Everything about the moment feels easy, beautiful, and right.

As the clock strikes twelve, everyone in the room removes their masks. Anticipating the sight of Charlie's eyes, she's shocked to discover that this whole time, her partner has been Ian.

She wakes up bereft. *I wanted it to be Charlie*, she thinks.

But it wasn't.

And, she realizes with sudden clarity, it will never be.

When Amy calls me in the morning, there's a conviction in her voice I haven't heard before. "Charlie will never have children, but I could never not. He isn't the one for me." She takes a breath. "I really care for Ian and he wants everything that I do. I'm going to give it a real try with him."

"And you're ready to let Charlie go?"

"It's time," she says with conviction. "I'm sad, but I'm ready."

Grief is to be expected when letting go of an ex—even if it's years after the fact. But a wise person once told me that the amount of grief we feel is directly proportional to how much we loved. "Maybe one day down the road," I say, "you'll be able to see past the grief and be grateful that your first love was a great one."

When we get off the phone, Amy sends Charlie a text:

*I can't be in touch with you anymore. Not because I don't love you, but because I love me. Thank you for being my first love. I wish only the most wonderful things for your life, especially that you find someone to share it with. You deserve that.*

His reply comes immediately: *I understand. Be happy, Ames. That's all I've ever wanted for you.*

Amy smiles to herself, then blocks Charlie's number and unfriends him on social media, per my advice. She's surprised how light that simple act makes her feel. Humming to herself, Amy takes a shower, makes a cup of coffee, and heads out into the sunshine to meet Ian for brunch.

## CHAPTER FIVE TIP

## Dating Detox Day-by-Day

### DAY 1

What does a Dating Detox mean to you? How long would you like your Dating Detox to be?

I, _____, am committing to a ____-day Dating Detox, during which time I will abstain from _____, while focusing on _____ and adding more joy to my life in the form of _____. I am choosing to do this for myself in order to realign my energy and approach dating from a renewed and refreshed place of groundedness and confidence so that I can attract my ideal soulmate. My Dating Detox begins today, _____.

### DAY 2

Make a list of your dating strengths and weaknesses. Identify the beliefs blocking your dating success. Identify which of the above you want to improve or work on.

### DAY 3

Today is all about identifying your dating baggage. What negative dating experiences have you had? What fears or emotional hang-ups do you have about the dating process?

### DAY 4

On any journey, you've gotta ask: What's making your baggage overweight? What do you need to unpack? The dating journey is no different. Today we'll be sorting all your baggage into three categories: carry-on baggage, regular baggage, and excess baggage.

Recognize how some of that baggage can be reframed to be helpful. Choose what baggage you can release.

## DAY 5

It's time to take control of your journey. Be honest about what would make your life exciting, with or without a partner. Identify what you've put on hold while waiting for a partner (e.g., a big move, investing in real estate or the stock market, an epic road trip, etc.). From the list you identify, what will you choose to take off hold in the next month?

## BONUS

Write down and clarify your new approach and attitude to dating. Make a dating plan. What will you do over the next thirty days to improve your dating? Build your support team. Who is on that list?

CHAPTER SIX

# The Secret of Attraction

Although Boston is technically a city, any native will tell you that it's really a big small town. Everyone knows everyone, which means that at a certain point, you'll probably have dated everyone. If you're lucky, one of those people will turn out to be your person. If you're not as lucky, like Scott, you could still be looking at age fifty-one.

For some bachelors, being single in your fifties may not feel like an emergency, especially if you're in Scott's position. He's the founder of his own successful marketing agency and the owner of a large condo in the cozy Brookline area. But for Scott, who grew up in a large family and has nieces and nephews who are now in high school, finding a partner is at the tippy-top of his priority list, code-red status.

The problem, he'll tell you, is twofold. First, he's a self-proclaimed "quirkburger" who has a unique sense of humor and a slight social awkwardness—though it only takes a few minutes in his company to see his warmth and kindness. However, many women don't stick around long enough to do so. The second issue is that he's run out of options. "I started dating seriously in my twenties, when I was still in college," he says. "Back then, there was a huge pool of women to choose from because Boston's a big college town. But no one was really thinking about settling down; they all had big plans for after graduation. Over time, the pool got smaller and smaller. People either moved away or got married or were focused on their careers. I grew up with most of the single women who are still in Brookline, and I promise you, I've gone out with all of them."

"Why not expand?" I ask. "Try someone from out of town?"

"Oh, I've done that, too. But I'm a Boston boy at heart. My whole family is here. My mother's house is two blocks away. I'm not willing to live anywhere else, and it's not easy to convince someone to pick up and move here for me."

The older he gets, the more women his age come with baggage. "They're divorced with kids, which means complications with the ex, or they've never been married but are so independent they don't know how to compromise."

"And you don't have baggage?"

"For sure, I do," he replies with a chuckle. "Single at fifty-one, a little weird, never been married, really attached to his family. What's wrong with this guy?"

"Absolutely nothing. My point is only that you need perspective when you're trying to find a partner. At this stage of the game, it's unrealistic to expect the same things you wanted at twenty-three. You may see certain things as liabilities, but you also have to look in the mirror and remember that you're coming with baggage, too."

"I understand. But what does it matter if there's no one left to date?"

"I'll bet there's someone hiding in the local woodwork we haven't found yet," I say. "We just have to look in the right place."

Until now, Scott has mostly dated women he's met through friends and family. He's dabbled in online dating, but it makes him nervous ("I've heard too many stories," he says). So I've decided to take the best of both options and use it to his advantage. We set him up with an account on a dating site, expanding his options exponentially. In just a few days, he comes across a suitable candidate: Michelle, a forty-seven-year-old art teacher living in Brighton, just two minutes from Scott's apartment.

"How have I never heard of her?" he asks.

"She only moved to the city from the North Shore last year," I explain.

"Oh—I know of her," he says with recognition. "She just moved here and wanted to get settled before she started dating."

Scott tries to cyberstalk Michelle's profile, but her account is private so he can only see a couple of photos. To fill in the rest, he'll have to meet her.

"Let's do it," he says.

## Date One

The chilly March rain has kept the crowds away from the Museum of Fine Arts this Sunday morning, which pleases Scott as he waits in the lobby for Michelle to arrive. Meeting here was Michelle's suggestion; she regularly comes on Sundays to get inspiration and ideas for her classes, and thought he might like to join her. Scott has been here before, of course, and though he wouldn't call himself an art fanatic, he does like the beauty and serenity of the building.

Scott immediately identifies Michelle the minute she walks through the door. She is all color: bright purple raincoat, teal fringed boots, and a neon Keith Haring umbrella she shakes out over the entryway carpet. Pulling off her hood, she reveals a head of auburn Botticelli curls.

She is, Scott notes with disappointment, not beautiful.

There is, however, something pleasant about her smile, which she flashes at him when he walks over to say hello. Scott helps her out of her raincoat, noticing the blues and greens of her sweater dress, which hugs her ample hips. The olive tones match her eyes.

"I guess you like color," he says.

"Would you believe I used to wear black all the time?" Michelle replies. "I was always told it would make me look smaller. But it made me *feel* smaller, too—and not in a good way. So after the divorce, I said, 'Forget it,' and started wearing what made me happy."

"How long ago was that?"

"About five years," she says. "Since then, I've been swapping out things I did to please other people for things that make me feel like . . . me."

She smiles and shrugs in a loose, easy way that makes Scott instantly relax.

"What else have you swapped out?" he asks, as they make their way into a room full of mummies and Egyptian artifacts.

"My job, for one. I was a CPA for my ex's company for almost twenty years. I was good at it, which I thought meant that I liked it. And since it was a family business, I thought I had no other choice. But then I realized that most people don't cry on Sunday night, dreading having to go to work the next day."

"I can relate," Scott replies. "I was at one of these huge, respected marketing agencies downtown where they've been using the same formula for fifty years. No innovation, no creativity. They had the same six ideas they recycled over and over again. It made me crazy. Finally, I decided to quit and go out on my own."

"And you're doing well, apparently," Michelle says. "Your website looks great."

"You've seen it?"

She cocks a playful eyebrow. "I do my research."

They head into the "Impressionism and Beyond" exhibit, where Michelle lights up as she explains the meaning behind

Gauguin's intriguing mural, *Where Do We Come From? What Are We? Where Are We Going?* Though not an art aficionado by any stretch, Scott can't help but be taken in by Michelle's enthusiasm. It's clear that she was meant to be a teacher.

By the time they sit across from the enormous Buddha sculpture toward the back of the museum, Scott feels as if he's catching up with an old friend; he finds himself telling Michelle things that he rarely talks about with other people. "I've never been the type who had a hundred friends," he admits, "just one or two people I like hanging out with. But my family is at the center of the Brookline community; even now, there are people constantly coming in and out of my parents' house. I always hated the crowds and the noise; I preferred to stay in my room. My mother used to ask me, 'Aren't you lonely?', which I wasn't, but it made me feel like I should be. Since then I've felt this pull between enjoying my close circle and feeling like I'm supposed to expand it. Do you know what I mean?"

Michelle sighs in solidarity. "*Supposed to*: two of the ugliest words in the English language. I think it's great that you have a close circle you like. Better to have one or two real friends than a hundred people who don't really know you."

Scott smiles in response. He's never felt more at ease with a woman before.

What a shame that he won't be going out with her again.

"What do you mean?" I ask, when Scott informs me of his decision. "You like her, don't you?"

"She seems like a great person, but . . . well . . . I'm not attracted to her."

"Are you repulsed by her?" I reply.

"Repulsed?"

"Does the thought of touching her make you want to gag?"

"No, no, nothing like that," Scott says.

"Okay, good. If that was the case, this relationship would be dead in the water. But if you're simply neutral about her, we have something to work with."

"But . . . I was hoping for better than neutral. Shouldn't the person I'm going out with get my blood going a little?"

"Just because she doesn't right now doesn't mean she never will."

In an age when everything from Wi-Fi to coffee is instant, we assume that attraction should be, too. Most of us have been raised on Hollywood romance, after all, where it takes just a single glance across a crowded room to turn up the heat. I'm not saying this is impossible; I know plenty of couples who were attracted to each other right away. However, you can also *cultivate* attraction. It just takes a little more time and energy.

"But what's the point of putting all that effort into something that might not work out?" Scott asks.

"If we go on that logic, then what's the point of putting in the effort with anyone?"

"Good point."

"There's clearly something here that's worth exploring further," I say. "Can we agree that you enjoyed being with her?"

"Yeah. I really did."

"Then you're already off to a good start. Here's the secret to attraction: it's about *way* more than just looks."

"So I shouldn't care about being physically attracted to my partner?" Scott asks.

"Of course not! Physical attraction and good chemistry are *musts* in a healthy relationship. If you're disgusted by someone, they're not for you. What I'm saying is that just because Michelle's looks aren't wowing you today doesn't mean they won't in the future."

"How is that possible?" he says. "Her looks aren't going to change."

"No, but the way you look at her will."

There was a point in my life when I was *really* into astronomy. It was exciting to search for and find the many constellations in the sky. But sometimes, I was stumped. No matter how hard I tried to find one, I couldn't see it. Then, someone would turn my head the right way or point out some nearby stars and then, suddenly, there it was. It had been right in front of me the whole time.

We can be like that with people, too, focusing on one miniscule detail when there is a much bigger and more beautiful constellation to discover. Maybe we're looking in the wrong direction or haven't given the search enough time. Maybe we don't even know what to look for. But then you change your position or find a few nearby stars and—voila!—like a miracle, a whole new image comes into view. When it comes to finding your person, it's the most important "Aha!" moment you'll ever have.

"Right now, you're concerned mostly with Michelle's appearance," I explain. "But looks are just one of a few main ingredients to attraction. And if you build up the other ones, she may look different to you as time goes on."

"Sounds like magic," Scott says.

"More like a combination of time and elbow grease. But the results can be magical."

Scott laughs. "You're one heck of a saleswoman. Alright. Tell me how it's done."

"Since we're already talking about looks, let's start there. Have you ever seen a male peacock on the hunt for a mate?"

"Sure, they fan out their feathers and show off for the ladies."

"Exactly. Our looks are designed to attract; that's why we spend a good part of our lives making ourselves as physically desirable as possible. This is great to get things going with a prospective partner, but a relationship can't live by looks alone. Even if you put two of the most gorgeous people on the planet together, if they have nothing else in common, the relationship will sputter out and die."

"I actually knew a couple like that," Scott adds. "My brother's best friend is really good looking. Both of my sisters had huge crushes on him when we were growing up. He married this stunning Brazilian woman, but they got divorced in less than a year. When I asked him what happened, he said, 'We had nothing to talk about.'"

"Yep," I say. "External attraction on its own has no staying power. You need internal attraction to feed it."

"But what if the external isn't there in the first place?"

"Excellent question, and exactly where I was headed. You're already on the right track."

Scott grins.

"Although nobody wants to hear it, the spark of attraction doesn't always start from the outside in," I say. "You can actually get the fire going from the inside out. So let's talk about Michelle's personality. From what you've told me, you're a big fan."

"That's true. She's smart and interesting, and she has this warmth about her that makes me feel much more comfortable with her than I do with most people."

"This is a very big deal," I reply. "You're already attracted to Michelle's personality—that is, the qualities and character traits that make up who she is. And unlike looks, personality doesn't sag." This, I explain, is actually the most stable indicator of a good match. "If her personality is attractive to you now, it will probably still be fifty years down the road."

That said, personality isn't strong enough to power 100 percent of attraction. You need values and beliefs to line up, too. "What we value and believe informs the choices we make and how we live our lives," I continue. "You can have two people with electric chemistry and a perfect personality match, but if their beliefs and values don't align, they might have fun together, but building a life that satisfies both of them will be next to impossible."

I tell him about Amy and Charlie, whom we met in the last chapter, whose values about having children didn't align. As we know, they adored each other, but it wasn't enough to make their relationship work.

"But beliefs and values change," Scott points out. "I used to believe plenty of things in my twenties that I don't believe now."

"You're right," I reply. "People adopt and discard beliefs all the time. I used to be a die-hard vegetarian, but I'm not anymore. If I'd married another vegetarian and we had nothing else in common, we'd be in big trouble."

(For the record, my husband might be the most carnivorous man on the planet. As I chat with Scott, Gershon is frying chicken. It's Tuesday morning.)

"That's why we need the *combination* of something static, like personality, with values and beliefs, which can be more variable," I continue. "The bottom line is compatibility. The more aligned you are in personality, beliefs, and values, the more compatible you are. And compatibility fuels attraction."

"A plus B equals C," says Scott, chuckling.

"You got it. But that's not the whole equation."

"There's more?"

"I like to keep my clients on their toes," I say. "Now, while alignment in some aspects is great for attraction, you need some misalignment, too."

"I'm not sure I'm following you."

"Okay," I say. "Tell me, Scott: what's something that really bothers you?"

"Hmmm . . ." Scott thinks for a minute. "I hate being late."

"Now imagine you were dating someone who was always twenty minutes late for everything."

"Oh, man. It would drive me crazy."

"Of course it would. That's what I mean by misalignment. Every human being has things that bother them. If the person you're dating triggers those bothers more than moderately, the relationship won't last long."

I tell him about a former client of mine who has misophonia, the hatred of certain sounds. Loud chewers made her want to reach across the table and stab them with her fork. "For obvious reasons, she steered clear of people who chew their food with sound effects."

"She wouldn't go out with me, then," Scott says, sheepish. "I've been told I'm a loud chewer. I guess I should work on that . . ."

"Absolutely, but that's not the point. What I'm trying to say is that the more someone triggers what bothers you—and it doesn't matter what those bothers are—the less likely the relationship will work."

"Okay, I think I got it. Alignment with personality, beliefs, and values, misalignment with bothers. Is that right?"

"Yep. Now there's just one last element we need to discuss: fear."

"Is this like a Freudian thing?"

I laugh. "Nothing so complicated. We all have fears of some kind; even if you spend years working through them, there are some that are here to stay. That's just part of being human."

"So what's the problem?" asks Scott.

"Nothing, as long as your person doesn't set them off. Fear is like a mine that can remain underground for decades without hurting anyone . . . unless someone steps on it. If you date someone who steps on yours, the connection will explode—and not in a good way."

"How scary can someone be already?" Scott says. "It's not like they're going to sneak around wearing a *Scream* mask or something."

"That's not the fear I mean. Have you ever seen *Sex and the City*?"

Scott blushes. "Possibly."

"So you'll know all about Carrie and Mr. Big. Personally, I'm not a fan of the show, but their relationship is the perfect example of how fears can kill a relationship. Carrie, like most human beings, wants to feel that Big cares for her and is committed to her. But he deliberately plays games with her emotions and makes her fearful to ask for what she really needs. Carrie never knows where she stands; he makes her feel unsteady and insecure. In the end he drives her so crazy, she has to break up with him."

(That she had to do so more than once says more about Carrie than it does about Big. If you run back to someone who you know triggers your fears, that's no longer a "them" problem; it's a "you" problem.)

"But is it really possible to find someone who doesn't trigger your fears at all?" Scott asks.

"Probably not. We're dealing with humans, after all. But if your fears are set off to only a low or average level, that's fine. The problem is when your partner regularly launches you into mayday crisis mode. With enough time, even the most gorgeous person can become unattractive—not because their looks changed, but because of the ugly way they treated you."

It's that old mosquito-versus-snake-bite scenario, I tell him: is it just a minor annoyance, or straight-up poison?

"Let's recap," I say. "You've got your five ingredients: looks, personality, values, fears, and bothers. There needs to be just the right measurement of each for the recipe to work. If you go too heavy on looks and too light on values, or overload the fears and skimp on the personality, the cake will fall flat."

"That sounds really complicated," Scott says, "and like a heck of a lot of work."

"Only if you need it to be perfect, which no relationship is. In the real world, we're looking for a solid match with personality and values, while fears and bothers stay mostly in the safe zone. If you have that covered, neutral-plus looks have a good chance of catching up—which is exactly the scenario I think you're in."

I see something click in Scott's eyes. "*That's* why you want me to keep going out with her."

"Now you're getting it," I say. "Instead of ruling out Michelle right off the bat because you're ambivalent about her looks, give yourself a chance to see how things line up in terms of values, fears, and bothers. Personality is already looking good; maybe everything else will turn out the same way."

"Okay," Scott concedes. "Let's say everything else does align. It doesn't mean that Michelle is magically going to turn into the hottest person I've ever seen."

"Well, most people don't marry the hottest person they've ever seen."

"What do you mean? Isn't that what you're supposed to think about your partner?"

"Come on, Scott. Let's get real. We're constantly bombarded with images of extremely hot people; unless you're blind or never look at another woman again, you will definitely see people who are hotter than she is. This is true even for hot people: there will always be someone hotter than they are. Shocker, I know. However, when you combine all the elements and build a true, deep connection, she will be the most beautiful person to you. It's not about how you feel when you look at her; it's about how she makes you feel when you're with her."

I remind Scott of my golden rule: *Assume this person is your spouse until proven otherwise.* "If she's not for you, you'll figure it out soon enough," I say. "But if you assume there's only dirt underground, you could miss a gold rush."

"Okay," Scott replies. "I'm in."

## Date Three

An unexpected snowstorm hits the city, wiping out Scott's plans to meet Michelle for dinner in the North End. "But I've got bread in the oven and a giant pot of soup on the stove," she says. "Why don't you join us for dinner?"

"Oh, Jake is with you tonight?"

"Yeah, his dad's away on business."

Scott deliberates. Michelle mentioned her son many times on their first two dates, but he hadn't expected to meet Jake so soon. "You sure he wouldn't mind me coming over?"

"Of course not," Michelle says with a laugh. "Jake's the one who told me to go out with you in the first place. He said he wants to check you out."

(Normally, I would never recommend introducing someone's child to a relationship this early on, but these are special circumstances. The weather has made it impossible for them to get together unless Scott comes to her, and Jake is happy about the situation. In other cases, if the kids are younger or have no idea that their parent is dating someone, I believe it's better to introduce them only when things are really serious.)

"Well," says Scott, "if it's okay with him, it's okay with me."

An hour later, after a quick, ten-minute walk through the quiet snowfall, Scott finds himself for the first time in Michelle's apartment. Like her wardrobe, the place is a burst of color: rich navy walls crowded with jewel-toned paintings and family photos, a deep emerald-green couch, throw blankets in purple and amber, magenta pillows. It should be chaos, yet somehow, it all fits together to create a warm, cozy atmosphere, especially with the smell of fresh bread coming in from the kitchen.

"You're here!" Michelle says, giving Scott a quick peck on the cheek. Her curls frame her face, which is flushed from cooking, and a streak of flour dusts her cheek. Something about this domestic image of Michelle makes Scott smile.

She calls over her shoulder, "Jakey! Scott's here! Come say hello!"

In strides Michelle's sixteen-year-old son, Jacob, wearing a T-shirt that says "#crueltyfree" and two AirPods in his ears. He's thin and lanky and a good head and a half taller than his mother, but the green of his eyes and his smile are Michelle's exactly.

The young man pushes back his shaggy black hair, removes one of the AirPods, and offers Scott a friendly wave. "Hey. I'm Jake."

"Scott. It's really nice to meet you. Thanks for letting me come for dinner."

"You're doing me a favor," Jake replies. "Maybe now we'll talk about something besides Cubism."

Michelle gives him a playful shove. "I do *not* always talk about art."

"That's true," Jake says. "Sometimes you talk about painters."

Michelle laughs and turns to Scott. "He's a trip, this one."

Scott grins. "I can tell."

"She'd be bored without me," Jake retorts, heading to the dining room to set the table.

Scott spends the next few hours in the delightful company of Michelle and her son, whose loving, joking connection with each other makes Scott feel right at home. As someone whose family is the center of his life, Scott appreciates the fact that Michelle has clearly given her all to raising Jake, a committed vegetarian and president of his high school's A/V club. In fact, Jake is one of the most personable, respectful, mature, and well-mannered teens he's ever met. When Scott mentions that he's never heard of Akira Kurosawa, Jake shows no sign of disdain; instead, he politely and passionately explains how the revered Japanese auteur combined western influences with eastern storytelling to create powerful, influential films like *The Seven Samurai*.

"I have crushes on artists," Michelle jokes. "He has crushes on directors."

Only once during the meal of tofu and cauliflower curry does a quick moment of light tension arise, when Michelle mentions that Jake is supposed to spend the weekend with his father.

"Even though I *told* him I already had plans to see Ashleigh's band play at Passim," Jake growls, roughly spearing a cube of tofu with his fork.

In plenty of other families, this could lay the seeds of an argument. But Michelle smiles placidly at him and says, "I'm proud of you for being honest with your father. I'm sorry that you won't be able to spend time with your friends, but I can understand why he doesn't want to give up his weekend with you. I live with you and I still want to see you every chance I can get."

Despite himself, Jake smiles back.

And just like that, the buoyant mood is restored.

Scott is deeply impressed. *She is a wonderful mother.*

From across the table, he locks eyes with Michelle, subtly tipping his head in acknowledgment. Michelle, sensing his message, grins back.

"Mom . . . are you blushing?"

Michelle snaps out of the moment as if from a daze, fanning herself with her hand. "What? No. Blushing? No," she stammers. "It's just hot in here, right? Maybe I left the oven on . . ."

In a flurry, she leaves the table for the kitchen.

Jake raises his water glass to Scott. "Nicely done," he says. "No one's ever made her blush before. Not even O'Keeffe."

## Date Five

"I can't decide between the pastrami and the hot turkey sand-wich," says Scott's sister, Renee, to him over the top of her menu. On the back is the logo of the Brookline deli where Scott and his family have been eating for years, which is as familiar to him as his sister's bright red hair.

Renee turns to her husband, Max, who wears his standard uniform of a polo and khaki shorts, even in winter. "What do you think?"

"I think you should get what you want," Max replies, not looking up from his menu.

Renee rolls her eyes. "That's the thing, Max. I don't *know* what I want."

"You still have a few minutes to decide," Scott says, checking his phone. "Michelle's just parking."

When Scott suggested to me that he and Michelle's next outing should be a double date with Renee and Max, I hesitated. Again, it's really early for Michelle to meet them.

"I get that you've already met Jake, so it's only fair for her to meet your family," I said. "But it's a risk."

"I know what you're saying," Scott replied. "It could mess things up if they don't like her. But I really value Renee's opinion; she knows me better than anyone. If she does like Michelle, I'll feel really good about it."

Without my telling him, Scott has already intuited a fundamental truth about attraction: the support of the right people can help kick it into high gear. People *love* to play matchmaker, especially for the ones they care about most. Even as a professional dating coach with many years of experience, I firmly believe that everyone could (and should!) be a matchmaker. Not only do we all have social and family circles that are ripe with potential connections, but we also see things in other people they might not be able to see for themselves. This is particularly true of family, who (for better or worse), know us better than anyone. So, assuming that your relationship with them is healthy and supportive, who better to help you find a partner? Not only will they be able to identify someone who is great for you, but when they see the beauty in the person you're dating, you'll be able to see it, too.

However, the wrong people can do the opposite, complicating things to the point of collapse. This is why I was concerned about bringing Renee in so soon. But once again, these are special circumstances. Scott and Michelle are not two kids in their twenties; they want to know sooner than later if it's going to work out between them. It was already risky for Scott to meet Jake, but it worked out well. Now they're taking another gamble, but in this case, it's probably a smart one.

As Michelle sweeps into the restaurant, Scott stands up to meet her. Renee stands up, too, enveloping Michelle into a hug when she reaches the table.

"I'm so happy to meet you!" Michelle says. "I've heard so much about you and your family."

"Scott's told us all about you, too," Renee replies. "But, Scotty, you didn't tell me how pretty she is!"

Renee's words, and Michelle's smile in response, shift something in Scott's brain, as if a blurry picture he'd been looking at suddenly comes into focus. Renee's right; Michelle really *is* pretty.

"What's everyone getting?" Michelle says, sliding into the booth next to Scott.

"Tuna melt," Max says, still surveying the menu.

"He always orders the tuna melt," Scott adds.

"I'm debating between the pastrami and the turkey," Renee says.

"Oooh, both sound good," says Michelle. "Why not get both and we'll share?"

"I love that idea! Hey, where did you get that scarf? The color is gorgeous."

"Thanks! I knitted it."

"You're a knitter?" Renee exclaims. "*I'm* a knitter!"

Although this was intended as a double date, it turns out to be a single date between Renee and Michelle, who fall in love with each other over their shared sandwiches, laughing and talking while Scott and Max look on in amusement. Scott doesn't mind in the slightest. One of his major fears is family conflict; seeing Michelle and Renee's burgeoning friendship quickly lays that fear to rest. Scott hadn't realized until now that he'd been holding his breath to see if this would work. Now that it has, he's surprised by how excited he feels.

He reaches under the table, takes Michelle's hand, and squeezes it.

By the end of the meal, Michelle and Renee have exchanged numbers and made plans to meet for coffee and a run to the knitting store next week. As they all walk out to the parking lot together, Renee hugs them both, then says, "Scotty, I love her and she's fabulous for you. You have my full blessing and a warning not to screw it up."

To Michelle she says, "And if he does screw it up, please promise you will still be my friend."

Michelle laughs. "Deal."

Max gives Michelle a friendly hug as well. "It's nice to see Scott looking so happy."

As Renee and Max walk down the block toward home, Michelle catches Scott staring at her.

"What is it?" she says, reaching up to her face. "Is there something . . . ?"

"No." He takes her hands away from her face and lays his own on her cheek. "You're just . . . lovely."

Her eyes sparkle. "Thank you, Scott."

And right there in the parking lot, he pulls her in for a kiss.

## Eight Months Later

"We're engaged!" Scott tells me over the phone.

"I guess things are going well, then." I reply with a laugh.

"Aleeza, I've never been happier. Almost everything's lined up: personality, values, fears, looks . . ."

"Looks? Really?"

"I know!" he replies. "Something just . . . changed. I can't believe there was once a time I thought Michelle was just okay. Now I think she's radiant."

"So I don't have to worry about the chemistry between you?"

He laughs and clears his throat. "No. You do not have to worry about that."

"I'm so glad. And what about the bothers?"

"That part's not perfect, but it's not terrible. She doesn't like that I watch TV late at night when she's trying to sleep, so I started wearing AirPods and she uses a sleep mask. My need to be twenty minutes early to everything also makes her nuts, but we're working it out. Michelle is pretty messy and disorganized, which is tough for a neat freak like me, but I figure we have so much else going for us, I can handle it. When we move to our new place next month, I'm going to hire a professional organizer and regular cleaning help to handle it for us."

"That's a great solution!"

"You know, Aleeza," says Scott. "It's crazy to me now that I was ready to give up on the first date. Look what I might have missed out on."

"That's what happens when you put in the time to dig," I reply. "You just might strike gold."

## CHAPTER SIX TIP

# How to Activate Intentional Chemistry

**From the beginning:** Invest yourself. There is no intimacy without honest, sustained effort.

**First three dates:**

1. Face your date and make eye contact.

2. PUT YOUR PHONE AWAY.

3. Demonstrate active listening: lean in and respond with nods, questions, and small comments that show you're engaged.

4. SMILE!

**Dates four through six:**

1. Make sure you are not Hungry, Angry, Lonely, or Tired (HALT) on your dates. Fill your own cup beforehand so you can focus on them.

2. Address your date by name to create verbal intimacy.

3. Genuinely compliment things you notice. ("I thought you were really gracious with our server, even though the service wasn't great.")

4. Spend time together at night.

**Dates seven through ten:**

1. Buy them a small token pertaining to something you know they like or care about.

2. Share your feelings, ideas, hopes, and dreams. Vulnerability brings people closer.

3. Do something that's new and different for both of you. This shared experience can help you bond.

CHAPTER SEVEN

# Reality Is Sexier than Fantasy

N o one knows more than Becca the perils of online dating. At first, she had assumed there was no better place to meet her match than the Internet; as a video game programmer from Austin, Texas, her comfort zone is online. Becca was bullied mercilessly in middle school for her height—she hit five foot nine at thirteen—and her thousands of freckles, so it's been her ammo to try and make herself "smaller" in both height and personality. Even today, at twenty-six, she tends to stick to the sidelines rather than thrust herself into the center of the action—effectively living as an NPC (non-player character) instead of a leading lady.

But online, Becca doesn't have to work so hard (or worry about her appearance). She can simply engage with people on her terms, thinking about what she wants to say before she says it and developing a rapport in a slow, thoughtful way. Many times, she's felt that "click" (pun intended) while getting to know someone online and gotten excited about their potential. But then she meets them in person, and . . . game over.

"Like this last guy I went out with," she tells me. "He was an audio engineer I connected with. Cute picture, interesting profile. We chatted online for a couple of weeks, talked on the phone a bunch of times. We really hit it off. But then we met in person and it just . . . fizzled."

"What do you think happened?" I ask.

"I'm not sure. It was hard to shift from online to real life. After ten minutes, we ran out of things to talk about. Maybe we already said it all on the phone."

"I doubt that. If there was a real connection, you would still have had plenty to talk about," I say.

I suspect there was already a disconnect before Becca met him in person, but the question is, where? Like all mysteries that need to be solved, I start at the most logical place: the beginning.

"Becca," I say, "can you show me your profile?"

Becca obliges, opening up an app on her phone. Her picture is nice, if a bit outdated; her hair is much longer now than it was in the picture. "Time to update your pic," I advise. "The more recent the photo, the better."

"Does my hair length really matter?" Becca asks, tucking a red lock behind her ear.

"You'd be surprised at how these little details can throw people off. I knew a woman who posted a picture of herself with long blonde hair. Then she decided to cut it short and dye it black, but she didn't update her profile. She connected with someone online, but when he met her in person, he didn't even recognize her. It really turned him off."

"Is that a little, you know, shallow?"

"Not in this case, because it wasn't about black hair versus blonde hair. It was about the fact that she presented herself as something she wasn't. It's hard to adjust your expectations or even trust someone when the profile doesn't match the person. That's why we want to limit the dissonance between online Becca and real-life Becca."

"In other words, what you see is what you get?" she says.

"Even better: reality is sexier than fantasy."

"But isn't that, like, the whole thing about fantasy? That it excites you?"

"Sure, but only temporarily. Fantasy is a balloon with a hole in it; eventually, it falls back down to earth. A short escape once in a while is healthy, but real relationships happen in reality. Instead of blowing air into a broken balloon, let them see what's exciting about the flesh-and-blood person you are."

"And if they don't find anything?"

"Then that's great! That means they're not for you. Now, let's look at your profile . . ."

I quickly skim what she's written: *26-year-old video game pro-grammer. Friends say I'm smart, funny, friendly, and adventurous. My cat's name is Chun-Li. If you know, you know.*

"You consider yourself an adventurous person?" I ask.

"Yeah, I think so."

"Cool. What's something adventurous that you did in the last three months?"

"Ummm . . ." she thinks for a minute. "I tried sashimi?"

"Okay," I say, turning from the screen to Becca. "The word 'adventurous' on its own usually suggests you're physically active. Is that what you meant?"

Becca laughs. "I'm a gamer. Typing is my cardio."

"So let's tweak this a bit. Is there another way you're adven-turous? Do you experiment with food or recipes? Are you open to new experiences?"

"Honestly? Not really."

"So then we're striking that word from the record. In fact," I say, ruthlessly holding down the Delete button, "we're starting all over from scratch."

Becca cringes. "Really? It's that bad?"

"It's not bad, just ineffective. What you've got here describes everyone and no one. There's nothing specifically *you* about it. When we're done, anyone who reads your profile will get a peek into the world of Becca."

When writing a dating profile (or almost anything, really), stick to the golden rule: show, don't tell. A list of attributes is like a skilled politician who uses lots of words but doesn't actually say anything. We want *sentences*, not a staccato line of adjectives separated by commas. Think of your profile like a book jacket that has to sell you quickly on the story inside. If the blurb for *Moby-Dick* said, "Guy looks for a whale in the Atlantic," I guarantee it wouldn't be the classic it is today. But when you describe "the battle between human and nature, man and beast, good and evil, and the inner obstacles we all must overcome," you've got a winner. (If you are not a strong writer, if your first language isn't English, or if you simply have a hard time putting your thoughts into words, I highly recommend asking or hiring someone with those skills to help you write your profile.)

In this vein, you also want to be careful with word choice, especially in a dating profile, when you only have so many words to use. To make your profile sing, you have to be precise, economical, and most importantly, honest with the words you use. "In your case, the word 'adventurous' isn't really true," I explain. "You just said you wouldn't consider yourself open to new experiences. If so, your profile gives the impression that you're something you're not."

"I guess I thought it would make me sound more . . . interesting."

"You already are interesting. But I get the feeling you don't think so."

"I don't," she admits. "I mean, I basically work, sleep, hang out with my cats, game, read, and order takeout."

"Being interesting isn't always about how much you do. It's also about how you look at the world. Isaac Newton didn't go out much, but the way he thought and experienced nature made him *really* interesting." (That said, even he didn't think he was so special: "I do not know what I may appear to the world," he said, "but to myself I seem to have been only like a boy playing on the sea-shore . . . whilst the great ocean of truth lay all undiscovered before me.")

I suspect that Becca has fallen into the trap that many people do when dating, either in-person or online: they present themselves as an idealized version of who they want to be instead of who they actually are. It's no wonder, then, that her dates fizzle out in person: Becca's online matches are expecting to meet someone else.

"This is a very human mistake," I tell her. "We all have versions of ourselves we want to be, and that's good. It gives us something to strive for. But we also have to acknowledge and appreciate who we are now, today."

"But what if who I am isn't, you know, good enough?"

"Good enough for who?"

"I don't know . . . everyone," she says.

"Ah," I reply. "You must mean the court of 'they.'"

"Who?"

"You know, those invisible judges we always ask ourselves about: 'What will *they* think?' 'What will *they* say?'"

"Right," Becca says. "Them."

"So, who are 'they'?"

"I have no idea."

"So, basically, you've decided that you're not good enough according to a measurement you don't know, determined by people you can't identify."

Becca laughs. "Accurate."

"Listen, Becca," I say. "We've all been told at some point in our lives that we're not smart enough, wealthy enough, entertaining enough, interesting enough, attractive enough, *whatever* enough. If you genuinely agree with that, go fix whatever you think is lacking. It's good to do things that improve your self-image. But being *good* enough is a decision you can make right now."

"What's the difference?"

"Pretend that the only judge here is you. Would you say, objectively, that you are a person worth knowing? Worth spending time with?"

"I mean, I spend all my time with me."

"And you enjoy your company?"

"Yeah, I'd say so."

"So, if *you* think you're good enough, isn't that good enough?"

"I guess it is," Becca says. "But, you know, I've still got a million flaws . . ."

"Of course you do. You're human. But focusing on them won't get you very far. Better to look honestly at who you are right now and own it, loud and proud."

An old Cherokee story describes a little boy with two wolves inside: one angry and one peaceful. When the little boy asks his grandfather which wolf will win, the grandfather replies, "The one you feed." Essentially, what you feed grows. If all you look at is what's "wrong" with you, you'll drown in your flaws. But if you shine the spotlight on all your great qualities, you can give yourself the most powerful makeover on the planet—free of charge.

This is especially important in dating. Many people feel the urge to broadcast and apologize for what's wrong with them, like a disclaimer. I beg you: don't. First of all, no one has ever sold a product by telling the customer why it stinks. Secondly, what you think is wrong with you isn't their business. They may not even *see* this glaring flaw that you find so unforgivable, and if they do, they might even think it's cute. Who are you to tell someone what they should and shouldn't like about you? Let them decide how they feel. (Spoiler: eventually, they *will* find something they don't like, but chances are it's not the thing you think it will be. That's why it's better to just save your energy and simply be yourself.) On the flip side, acknowledge that you will also find something you don't like about your partner. No one is perfect; you can only work to see if your strengths and flaws are compatible with the other person's strengths and flaws.

"Being real is your superpower," I say. "The more real you are, the happier you'll be, and the easier it will be to find someone who fits you."

I tell Becca about an old client of mine who, despite the instinct to portray himself as tough and manly in his profile, decided to stick with the truth: "I'm a wimp when it comes to spicy food."

"This is spectacular," I tell Becca. "It's self-aware, honest, and lighthearted. This guy knows who he is and said so with no shame. And that's what you're going to do, too."

"But won't that scare some people off?" asks Becca.

"Yes! And that's great! You don't want to attract everything. More isn't better. More accurate is better."

Writing a dating profile is essentially marketing yourself. But unlike traditional marketing, which casts a big net to catch as many fish as possible, you want to *rule out* as many incompatibles as you can right away so that only the potentials stick. "Your profile should be high-value bait for someone on your wavelength," I say. "If they want more after reading it, you know you've got a live one."

"So let's get down to it," I say. "The best profiles don't give you the whole story, but give you random, rich bites of information that can quickly spark a connection—or kill it. So tell me something you really love."

"Umm . . . my cats?"

"Okay. What do you love about them?"

"I love when they curl up in my lap while I'm working and purr against my belly. It's really warm and comforting."

"Bingo," I say, typing. "This is *exactly* what I meant."

Instead of boring, vague adjectives that could describe anyone (*Funny? Funny how? Sarcastic? Goofy? Dry?*), this personal, sensory experience is a window right into who Becca is. Clearly, she loves cats, but she also appreciates the affection, comfort, and physical connection they offer. This tells you volumes about the kind of partner she'd be—and the kind of partner she wants—much more than a dry-as-toast list of her age, body type, location, or degrees ever could. It's also an instant connection point for anyone reading it. You can easily imagine a kitty curled up and purring on your lap. If the thought makes you want to crawl out of your skin, chances are that someone like Becca might not be a fit for you. But if it makes you sigh with contentment, congratulations: you and Becca already have something in common.

"Tell me more," I urge Becca. "What are other things you love? Or can't stand?"

"I hate running."

"Really? When did you run?" I type furiously.

"One New Year's I decided to train for a marathon. I went for my first practice run and realized it was a terrible idea."

I laugh out loud. "Yes!"

And so we continue for about an hour, when Becca's new profile is finally complete:

*You could say I'm a bundle of paradoxes. I'm a high-level gamer (which I turned into a career), but a failed marathoner. Though I'm a Texas native, country music is banned from my house. I love a purring kitten in my lap, but tickling is a hard no. I tried to impress my middle-school crush by stealing a tube of ChapStick from CVS, but I felt so guilty I returned it.*

"*This* is a dating profile with a hook," I say. "Now let's see who bites."

## Date One

Right before Becca enters Dirdie Birdie, the restaurant and mini-golf course, she gives herself a long look in the window. Before arriving here, she spent an hour getting on her "dating armor": straightening her thick hair, making up her face, pouring herself into a sundress, and cramming her feet into kitten heels. She's not exactly comfortable, but that isn't the point. She's created the Becca dating avatar that's more "feminine" and "sexier" than real-life Becca. She gives her reflection a tentative smile and walks in the door.

Becca's date, Michael, is already inside. She recognizes him right away from the scruffy beard in his profile picture. Instead of playing coy with online chatting, Becca agreed to meet him in person right away. She's a little disappointed by what she finds; Michael is less attractive and a little goofier than she expected.

As she reaches out to shake his hand, he notices the Pokémon keychain on her wrist.

"Pikachu! Nice!" Michael exclaims when he sees it. "When I was a kid, I wanted to be a Pokémon hunter. Now I'm a land-scape architect."

"Not far off," she jokes.

"Yeah, but instead of a Poké Ball, I have a Sharpie and a lawn mower."

Becca is relieved by the ease of their conversation and how much they have in common. Michael thinks it's "so cool" that she codes video games for a living; he loves gaming himself but doesn't have much time for it now that he's started working for a major landscaping firm. They've just put him on a project at UT Austin. "It's really fun and nostalgic for me, since I went to school there," Michael says.

"So did I!" Becca says.

"No way! How old are you?"

"Twenty-six."

"I'm twenty-seven! I can't believe we were there at the same time! Did you know . . . ?"

And so they spend the next hour playing "Who do you know?", eating tacos and drinking beer, and failing miserably at mini-golf. Michael is a polite and easygoing date, but Becca, while trying to ignore the pinching sensation in her feet, can't muster up more than appreciation for his company.

After returning their clubs to the front, Michael pays the bill and walks Becca to her car. "This was really fun," he says. "I'd love to hang out again sometime."

And with a friendly wave, he leaves.

*That's it?* she thinks.

For someone who was expecting fireworks, this date has been rained out.

"I don't get it," she tells me on the way home. "I was authentic in my profile. Wasn't he supposed to be the perfect guy?"

"First of all, there is no perfect guy, only someone perfect for *you*," I reply. "Second of all, being authentic in your profile isn't an instant fix-it. It's just a tool you use to narrow down your options. More important is being authentic in real life."

Changing Becca's profile is only the beginning, I explain. Now she has to rewrite her dating code from scratch. "This is about dating as real-life Becca, not virtual Becca. Remember: reality is sexier than fantasy."

"You mean, like, ditch the heels that are killing my feet?"

"If you don't normally wear heels, don't wear them on a date. Wear what makes you feel like you. Not that you should show up in your pajamas, but attractively comfortable."

"Feels weird," Becca says, "but I'll do my best."

## Date Three

No event in the history of Austin has excited Becca more than the Anime Film Festival. Normally, she would never invite a date to go with her, too fearful they might laugh at her for nerding out over Japanese animation. But in her quest to be more authentic, she buys two tickets and invites Michael to join her.

"Sounds fun," Michael says. "But I don't know anything about anime."

"Don't worry, I'll tell you anything you want to know. Probably a lot more than you want to know."

Becca arrives at the Austin Film Society Cinema in distressed black jeans, sneakers, a vintage "Legend of Zelda" T-shirt, and a thrift store cardigan. Instead of wrestling with her hair, she's thrown it into an easy, messy bun on top of her head. And she has never felt more comfortable.

"Hi, there," Michael says, giving her a hug hello. "Nice shirt."

"Thanks!" she replies.

Looking around at the crowd, he says, "Sure I'm not an imposter here?"

She holds up the tickets. "Not if you have one of these."

As they watch a remastered version of *Princess Mononoke*, one of Becca's all-time favorite movies, she leans over to explain references to other films, fill in history, and provide random trivia. "You could teach a class," he whispers.

"Sorry . . . am I bothering you?"

"Not at all. I feel like I'm going to leave here ten times smarter than when I came in."

After the movie they go out for Pho at a restaurant not far from Michael's house. As always, the conversation is easy, fun, and playful—especially when Michael's soup turns out to be a lot spicier than he'd expected. They both laugh as he tries to cool his palate with cup after cup of tea.

It's clear to Becca that Michael really enjoys her company, but for the first time, she's paying attention to how *she* feels. As the evening goes on, Becca realizes that although she's having a great time, she feels no butterflies, no anticipation, no desire. She could just as easily have been hanging out with one of her girlfriends.

As they say goodnight, the moment comes when Michael could lean in to kiss her. Instead, he gives her a peck on the cheek.

In theory, she should be disappointed. But all she feels is relief.

"Okay, this doesn't make any sense," Becca tells me. "Great guy, great time. What the heck is wrong with me?"

"Nothing," I reply. "But your expectations may need some adjustment."

Expectations are sneaky little devils because wherever they begin is never where you end up. If your expectations are up, the only way to go is down. In Becca's case, she expected that since she's dating differently now, she would have instant success with

Michael. Naturally, she's disappointed that she feels only luke-warm about him. Reality: 2, Fantasy: 0.

Some people keep their expectations at rock bottom, knowing that they can only go up. That can protect you from disappoint-ment, but it can also make it harder to see the good in front of you. Other people try to temper their expectations by keeping them somewhere in the middle, but the risk is that they can go up or down. I've seen people ride the expectation roller coaster until they're dizzy and their clarity is completely skewed. Which is why, when it comes to expectations, I stick with only one rule: *You're my spouse until proven otherwise.*

"I once had a history teacher who told us on the first day of school, 'Y'all have an A. Now you just have to keep it,'" I tell Becca. "It was a totally different approach to school; we started out as winners instead of having to prove we were capable. It's the same thing with dating. Most people go into relationships looking for reasons why their partner isn't right for them. And what you seek, you shall find. But what if you assumed that Michael was your person until proven not? Maybe you wouldn't feel so much pres-sure to feel butterflies right off the bat."

"But what if he *isn't* my person? Doesn't that mean I'm forcing something that isn't there?"

"Don't worry; if he's not for you, you'll know it soon enough. It's not about forcing anything; it's about looking for what's right instead of what's wrong."

"That's the thing. Nothing is wrong, except that I feel *meh* at best."

"Good. Keep that information in your pocket. But don't rule out anything—or judge yourself—because of it. Maybe things will change, maybe they won't. Just keep your eyes open and see where it goes."

## Date Five

On their fifth date, Michael invites Becca to go ice skating at Northcross Austin. Becca, who took figure skating lessons as a kid, feels at ease gliding around the rink. Mike, on the other hand, has only been here once before and spends more time sitting on the ice than skating on it. They laugh a lot as Becca guides him around the arena, Mike's hand against the plexiglass, and at one point he falls and takes her down with him.

"Nine-point-eight from Austria," Mike jokes.

Something about the way he says it reminds Becca of her friend Melissa, who is also a little goofy and very smart. *They'd make a good match*, she thinks. Then she shakes the thought away.

*Why am I thinking of setting up my date with someone else?*

"What do you think?" I ask her when she checks in.

"I think . . . I think it means that he's not for me."

"You're absolutely sure?"

"I am sure, but I don't want to be. I don't want this to be another no."

"I hear you," I tell her. "But there's a blessing in a no. It means you're one person closer to your person."

"But why does it only have to be one person? Why can't I have, like, ten good options to choose from?"

Can you imagine a row of ten fantastic suitors in front of you, all a perfectly good match, and you get to choose the one you want? Sounds lovely in theory. In reality, it's a nightmare. How could you possibly choose? Each package is better than the next. It would be impossible to choose one and feel fully confident that you were making the right decision. God does us all a favor by only giving us one, maybe two, solid options.

"Have you ever been in this situation before?" I ask Becca. "That you knew someone wasn't right but you tried to make it be right?"

"Welcome to my last relationship," she replies. "I knew from the second date it wasn't a fit but I really wanted it to work. I stayed with him for six months until I couldn't take it anymore."

"And was it worth it?"

"No. I wasted my time. And his."

Reality: 3; Fantasy: 0.

"You've let fantasy guide you in your dating life until now," I say. "Fantasy profile, fantasy relationship. You've done a really good job trying to date in reality. Maybe part of this process is being real with yourself about how you feel."

Becca sighs. "There's nothing wrong with Mike. He's a really good guy."

"But maybe there's nothing right, either," I say.

"Yes! Exactly. Nothing wrong but nothing right. It sucks, but it's true."

"Good for you, Becca."

"I do think, though, that he'd be right for Melissa."

I grin. "Now you get to play matchmaker!"

A week later, Becca gets a text from Melissa.

*Just got back from my date with Mike. He's amazing! Thank you, thank you, thank you.*

*My pleasure!* Becca replies.

*It's so funny because I saw him online,* Melissa writes. *I was actually going to ask Katie to set me up with him, but when I heard you were dating him I backed off. I know I may not be able to return the favor, but I would like to try. There's this guy I went out with who I think might be good for you . . .*

## CHAPTER SEVEN TIP

Talking out your thoughts and feelings while dating is important—but only if you do it with the right people. Someone with their own agenda might try to push you in a certain direction, while too many opinions could drown out yours. Stick with one or two trusted people, such as a mentor, spiritual guide, parent, or a *married* friend to help you. (You know I love singles, but they've got the same questions and concerns that you do!)

Now, assuming you've picked the right people, **when should you spill your guts?**

1. Twenty-four hours after a date, when you're already clear about how you think and feel.

2. Twenty-four hours after a date, when you're still unsure, but with the clear boundary that you want them to simply listen and reflect without opinions.

3. When you're excited and you want someone to celebrate it with!

**When should you zip your lip?**

1. When you're at the height of an emotion and easily triggered. Go for a walk, meditate, or do something else to let off steam before you bring them into the picture.

2. When you are tempted to share private information about the other person that was only meant for your ears. In that case, speak with a therapist.

3. When you've already spoken to multiple people and there are too many voices in your head.

4. When they want something different for you than what you want for yourself.

# CHAPTER EIGHT

# Do the Math

In the ballroom of Miami's Four Seasons Hotel, a legendary bat mitzvah is underway. With the theme of "Paris in the Springtime," the room has been transformed into the magical French city, with a ceiling-high model of the Eiffel Tower, cobblestone streets, a Moulin Rouge, and even a small "Seine" burbling through. Hundreds of guests sit outside "cafes" and "patisseries," enjoying smoked salmon canapés, mini onion galettes, and baguette slices with Brie and Camembert. French lavender scents the air, while the sounds of a jazz band, accompanied by a singer that sounds eerily similar to Edith Piaf, fill the room.

On guard near the Arc de Triomphe (and the entrance to the kitchen) is Joely, forty, wearing a simple black cocktail dress, red lipstick, and a headset over her ears. There's a professional smile on her face, but the focus of her gaze and the square of her shoulders suggest that she means business. As well she should: as the founder of Eventt, one of Miami's most sought-after event planning agencies, Joely is the captain of this entire operation.

"Cue the fountain," she says into the headset, while casually grabbing the arm of a passing waiter holding a tray. "Canelés don't come out until *after* the main course," Joely tells him. As the waiter about-faces to the kitchen, Joely beckons to the wine steward. "More champagne at the host's table," she murmurs in his ear, never breaking her smile.

As the steward heads off, Joely feels a tap on her shoulder. At her side is a stocky, handsome man in a tuxedo, his thick dark hair graying at the forehead and temples. "Hi," he says.

"Can I help you with something?" Joely says with professional courtesy.

"I can see you're very busy," the man says, "so I won't interrupt you for long. My name is Drew. I'm an uncle of the bat mitzvah girl."

She shakes his hand. "Joely. I'm the event planner."

"I know. I've been watching you orchestrate this thing for the last two hours. I'm very impressed. This is a major production and you haven't lost your cool once."

"I've been at this a long time," she replies, her eyes tracking a moving object over his shoulder. "I don't mean to be rude, but if there's nothing I can do for you . . ."

"Of course. I was hoping, maybe when you're not on duty, I might take you out sometime?"

Now Joely's eyes lock on his. "Oh! Um . . ."

"No need to decide now," Drew says, slipping a business card into her hand. "Take this, and if you want to go out, you know where to reach me."

"Thanks," she says, and slides the card into her pocket.

Drew heads back to his table, and within six seconds, Joely forgets the conversation.

That is, until two weeks later, when she picks up her black dress from the dry cleaners and finds Drew's business card stapled to her receipt.

Had it been any other time, Joely would have probably thrown the card away. Despite the fact that Drew seemed like a decent guy—confident, charming, no lame pickup lines, looked her right in the eye—he's not exactly her type. But Joely's forty-first birthday came and went last week, and though she had a lovely dinner out with her family, she felt herself longing for a partner to celebrate with her. *Maybe,* she thinks, *it's time to try something different.*

Joely drives home, hangs the dress in her closet, plops into a chair in her living room, and, finally, calls Drew.

A month later, Joely and Drew walk hand in hand through the Berry Farm Harvest Festival. Joely has never been the hand-holding type, but with Drew, it feels different. Right. She never thought she'd date someone like him, yet here she is, surrounded by the idyllic nostalgia of fall, in the company of a man who is clearly taken with her.

In the time since they started dating, their relationship has progressed with an ease that has taken Joely by surprise. Drew is kind, steady, and attentive to Joely. He was married once for a short time right after college, but as he explains it, "We were both too young." They divorced with no children, and Drew went to work for the family trucking company. After his father passed away, Drew and his brother, David (host of the bat mitzvah), took over the company, which is where Drew has devoted most of his energy for the past fifteen years. But more recently, he's started to think about settling down with a partner. "David's been giving me a hard time about it for years, but I didn't start taking it seriously until I turned forty," he says. "Now I really want to build a home life."

Joely has mentioned that her last relationship ended a few years ago, but beyond that, she hasn't said much. She has, however, told him all about her parents, Cuban immigrants who started out selling beauty products from their basement and who now own a well-known beauty supply chain in South Florida; her sister, a homemaker with three kids who lives in Coral Gables; and her brother, a Los Angeles–based composer for commercials and television shows. Joely has never been so forthcoming about her family before; it's a good sign, she thinks. But deep down, she suspects she's also buying time by sticking to a safe topic. Eventually, if things get more serious, she knows she's going to have to tell him more about her history.

But in the meantime, they enjoy the fair, walking contentedly past booths hawking pumpkin-spice everything, bruising their behinds on a hayride, getting lost and finding each other in a corn maze, and munching on candy apples while a local band plays '90s hits. Around them are a multitude of families, and children's squeals and laughter fill the air.

As they emerge from a sunflower field, Joely hears someone calling her name. "Joely! Joely! Is that you?"

Joely turns to see a blonde woman in jeans and a peasant blouse with a baby in a sling on her chest. "Bea?!?" Joely exclaims. "Oh, my gosh! I can't believe it!"

Joely and Bea embrace.

"*Look* at you!" Joely gushes. "You're a mom!"

Bea runs a hand over the baby's head. "Yep! This is Theo. And this—" she gestures to the smiling, dark-haired woman beside her "—is my wife, Maggie."

"Maggie!" says Joely, hugging her as well. "It's lovely to meet you."

"Same here," says Maggie.

Joely hears Drew subtly clear his throat beside her. "I'm so sorry!" Joely says, placing a hand on his arm. "I was just so surprised to see . . . Bea, Maggie, this is Drew. He's . . ." She falters for a moment, unsure of how to introduce him.

"We're dating," Drew covers smoothly, offering his hand.

At the word "dating," Joely notices a surprised look pass between Bea and Maggie, but Bea recovers quickly. "Pleasure," she says. "How long have you two been together?"

"Not long," Joely says.

"Month and a half," Drew adds.

"Interesting," Bea says, her eyes darting from Joely to Drew and back again. "Well, it was really nice running into you, Joely. You look great."

"So do you! Marriage and motherhood really suit you."

Bea and Maggie smile at each other. "Thanks," says Bea. "See you around."

"Yep," Joely replies. "See you."

Bea and Maggie walk off together hand in hand, the picture of domestic bliss. Joely watches them for a moment before Drew's voice pulls her back into the present.

"You okay?" he says.

"Yeah, yeah," Joely replies, turning back to him. "That was just the last person I expected to see today."

"How do you know her?"

Joely takes a deep breath. "I almost married her."

When Joely was sixteen, she realized she was attracted to both men and women. It was a confusing time for her; back in the '90s, there wasn't much (healthy) dialogue about sexuality in general, let alone a space for LGBTQIA+ people to explore or express themselves openly. Her parents were loving people, but it wasn't until she'd left for college and had a few relationships that Joely felt confident enough to come out to them. It was difficult for them to understand, and her mother admitted that she was disappointed, which hurt Joely deeply. It took a number of years for everyone to heal and adjust, but eventually their relationship came back into balance. However, it left Joely with profound empathy for LGBTQIA+ people who did not have the support of family, friends, or community—or who had maybe lost such support after coming out. She became highly involved in LGBTQIA+ activism, protesting for civil rights and against discrimination, and serving as a mentor and advocate for young people in crisis. After the 2016 shooting at the gay club, Pulse, in Orlando, Joely helped organize a drop-in center in Miami where anyone who needed a space to process and grieve was welcome.

It was through this project that Joely met Bea, another activist, and as people do in times of crisis, they bonded quickly. However, their attraction outlasted those brief months; after two years as a couple, they started discussing the prospect of marriage. The problem, however, was that Bea was ready to start a family immediately. Joely, on the other hand, was ambivalent at best about kids. It was this impasse that eventually led to their breakup.

Bea had been the only person with whom Joely had ever considered a real future. Without her in the picture, the next chapter of Joely's life was murky, unclear. So when Drew showed up, she was surprised by how well they fit together. Though she'd always looked for a person, not a gender, after years of deep immersion in the LGBTQIA+ community, it still surprised Joely that she could begin envisioning a future with a man. Like someone slowly immersing in cold water, Joely was just starting to get comfortable with the idea. She planned to tell him everything soon, but then . . . they'd run into Bea and Maggie.

"I wasn't *not* telling you," Joely assures him, "it just . . . hadn't come up yet."

"You mean you weren't ready?" Drew replies.

She nods in agreement.

"Listen," Drew says, taking her hand. "I wish you'd told me sooner—"

"I know, I'm sorry . . ."

"—but I understand why you held off. It's a big thing. I get it."

"So you're not upset?"

"I'm surprised," Drew says. "I sensed you had something to tell me, but I didn't know it was that."

Joely's eyes tear up. "I understand if you want to end it."

"Why would I end it? You're fantastic. What's past is past. As long as you're in it with me now, we're good."

"Really?" she says.

"Really."

Joely smiles at him. "You're a good guy, Drew."

"Nah," he says. "I just wanted the rest of your apple cider doughnut."

Since that conversation, Drew has said all the right things. He's asked questions out of respect and a genuine desire to understand Joely better. He's been supportive and encouraging. By all accounts, she could not have gotten a better, more promising reaction. Yet, ever since that day at the festival, thoughts of Bea's and Maggie's surprised faces play on repeat in Joely's head. She begins questioning herself and the relationship, and anxiety starts creeping in. Slowly, she begins to withdraw from Drew. Instead of that warm feeling she got holding his hand, now she simply feels cold whenever he touches her. Instead of looking forward to seeing him, Joely has started looking for excuses to avoid him. Perhaps that's why she throws herself so deeply into planning the annual fundraising gala for a local LGBTQIA+ organization; it distracts her from her conflicting feelings. It's frustrating and confusing for Joely, who knows intellectually that Drew is fantastic, and that underneath the icy surface layer over her heart, she really does care for him. For this reason, she doesn't break things off with him; instead, she prays that this is just a phase that will pass soon enough.

But it's not until one night when Drew is at her apartment that Joely realizes what a problem it's become.

"Is this the invitation for the gala?" he asks, eyeing a colorful card on her fridge. "It's really nice."

Joely is instantly uneasy. "Thanks."

"Why didn't you tell me it was coming up so soon?"

"I thought I did," she replies vaguely.

"Nope," says Drew. "That's okay, though. If I have anything on the twenty-third, I'm sure I can move it."

"You don't have to."

"Why not? You have another date lined up?"

Joely laughs lightly. "No, I'm just going to be really busy. You'll probably spend most of the night alone."

"That's okay. I like watching you do your thing."

He reaches out to push a stray hair off her face. Without realizing it, she turns her cheek away from his hand.

"Really, Drew, it's fine," she says, with more of an edge than she intended. "You don't have to come."

He regards her for a moment. "I don't have to, or you don't want me to?"

"That's not what I meant."

"You sure about that?"

Joely feels a desperate push-pull in her chest, between the desire to hold on to him and, simultaneously, to push him away. "I do want you to come," she begins, "but maybe . . . it's better if you don't."

"I see."

"I don't know why I . . ." Joely shakes her head in frustration. "I'm sorry."

"Me, too," Drew says. "I'm pretty tired. I think I'll head home."

"You don't have to go . . ."

But before she can finish, he's grabbed his keys and walked out of her apartment.

And Joely, after a good cry, picks up the phone and dials my number.

"I don't know what it is," she says, her voice hoarse with emotion. "He's amazing. Like, really amazing. I don't understand why I'm pushing him away."

"I'm glad you called me before you did anything drastic," I reply. "Let's get to the bottom of this so you can make a choice you'll be deeply satisfied with."

Joely sniffs. "Okay."

"First of all, I want to make it clear that I don't specialize in LGBTQIA+ relationships," I say. "I have a lot of respect for your community and I know that there are nuances that I don't understand. I'm not going to pretend that I know something I don't. But I do think, with my expertise in heterosexual relationships, that I can help you with Drew."

"I appreciate that," Joely replies.

"Just so I'm clear, before that day at the fair, things were going well between you?"

"Really well."

"And has anything changed on his end since then?"

"Not that I can tell," she says. "He says all the time how much he wants to be with me and cares for me. It's me who's off."

"Off how?"

"I just can't access those feelings I had for him before. When he comes close, I want to take a step back—and I want to pull him closer."

"Did he do something that would make you feel this conflict?"

"Not at all. He's doing everything right." she sighs. "Maybe that's part of the problem."

"Drew doing everything right is a problem?"

"No, no. I love being with Drew. He's everything I've ever wanted in a partner. The problem is that I never imagined a partner like him—meaning, a straight man."

"But you told me yourself that you've always looked for a person, not a gender," I counter. "So why is it an issue if that person is a man?"

"It's not. I've dated men before. But this is the first time I've ever considered a real future with one."

"Why do you think it's different with Drew?"

She thinks for a minute. "Because he's a good person. There's no games, no drama. He's grounded. He's caring. He's open with his feelings. He makes me laugh."

"So in terms of personality, it's a great match."

"Absolutely," she agrees.

"What about Drew's values? Do you see some alignment there?"

"For sure. We're both ready to settle down with a partner and build a life together. And it's important to both of us to do something meaningful. Like, once a year, Drew donates all kinds of camping materials—tents, sleeping bags, folding tables, cooktops—to this organization for siblings of kids with terminal illnesses, and he drives it up there with a few of his guys in their trucks. It's the highlight of his year."

"And what about kids? You said that you and Bea broke up because you weren't ready to have them. Do you still feel that way?"

"I do," Joely admits, "I thought maybe things would change, but I have no real desire to go down that road."

"And Drew's okay with that?"

"We haven't really gotten into it, but I get the sense that he's in the same camp."

"I think you need to get more clarification on that," I reply, "but in general, can we say that your values are pretty simpatico?"

"Yes."

"Okay. So let's do the math."

I have developed a simple equation that determines whether a relationship has staying power: personality + values = compatibility ($p + v = c$). If $p$ and $v$ both have solid alignment (let's say, 70 percent or higher), the value of $c$ increases. If not, $c$'s value drops. In Joely's relationship with Bea, for example, they had great $p$ alignment, but a $v$ mismatch when it came to having kids. Hence, their breakup. However, based on what Joely is telling me about her $p$ and $v$ with Drew, their $c$ is off the charts.

"So you've never imagined a relationship like this before," I say. "When you do the math, it all adds up."

"Right, but maybe it doesn't add up with *me*," Joely counters. "Ever since I saw Bea and Maggie . . . I feel like an imposter."

"Tell me more about that," I say.

"The LGBTQIA+ community has been my other family for over twenty-five years," she says. "It's a huge part of who I am. I just assumed my long-term partner would fall into that picture. To choose a heteronormative relationship after all this time feels like I'm failing my community. Like I'm defecting or something."

"I'm sure you've talked to some of your friends in the community about this," I say. "What do they have to say?"

"They've been really supportive—my best friend, Mitchell, especially. He was like, '*Hello*, Joely, you're bi. Just because you haven't dated a man since *Gilmore Girls* was on the first time doesn't mean he's not technically your type.'"

I laugh. "Good point. Clearly, your friends know you."

"That's for sure!"

"Okay. So if the issue isn't with the community or with Drew . . ."

"Then it's with me," she says. "I was afraid of that."

"Nothing to fear. If you're the source of the problem, you're also the source of the solution. So let's get down to business."

Joely's main obstacle is timing—not in terms of how hers aligns with Drew's, but where Joely stands on her own timeline. Instead of looking forward to a future with Drew, Joely is looking backward and knocking herself off course. I call this "Past, Present, and Future Syndrome."

We all have different versions of ourselves: who we once were, who we want to be, and who we actually are. These are all important aspects of our identities, but the challenge is keeping them in balance. Plenty of people, for example, let past events dictate who they are—a trauma victim, for example, or an NHL all-star—then dedicate their present and future to reliving that experience. Others are so dissatisfied with their present selves or circumstances that they live entirely for an imagined future when everything will be perfect and wonderful. Still others are so afraid of the future that they retreat into the past.

When you're too focused on either past, present, or future, you risk missing the gifts that each has to offer. You cheat yourself out of becoming your truest, most authentic self. A healthy balance comes when you can look unflinchingly at the past, be present in the present, and plan realistically (and optimistically!) for the future.

"Your past experiences have shaped who you are today," I tell Joely. "That's important. But you can't let it block your present and sabotage your future, just because the person you found isn't what you imagined. It's easy to blame your crisis on the fact that Drew is a man, but the fact is that Bea is the only person you've ever envisioned a future with. I bet you'd still be feeling this way even if your partner was female, just because you've never considered anything else."

Put more simply, Joely's relationship adds up; it's she who's out of alignment.

I tell her about a client of mine who spent fifteen years in academia and was about to earn tenure at a reputed university when he decided to quit. He had always wanted to work with his hands and is now a master welder. "Imagine if he'd said, 'But I've always been an academic; I can't pivot now.' He'd still have a good job, but something would be missing."

"No one's telling you to abandon your past," I continue. "But you have to acknowledge who you are and what you want now, in the present. So far, Drew seems to have what you want; the math adds up. So keep exploring this. If it really is right, it will only feel better and better as you let him into your life. And if it doesn't add up in the long run, it will become clear."

"Okay," Joely says. "I'll do my best."

I leave her with an assignment: write down her feelings after every conversation or date with Drew. Like a researcher compiling evidence, this will help her get clear on what's really happening.

Three weeks later, Joely enters the archway of the Vizcaya Museum and Gardens, venue of the fund-raising gala that she has helped plan. The front hall, romantically lit with thousands of sparkling lights, looks stunning.

"Isn't it gorgeous?" she gushes.

"Yes," Drew replies, looking directly at her.

Joely blushes.

The morning after our conversation, Joely called Drew to apologize and share her thoughts with him. "I care about you so much," she said. "Like, more than I've ever cared about anyone, maybe even Bea. I just never imagined I would meet someone like you, or that it could get so serious, so quickly. It's a little scary."

"I'm with you," Drew replied. "I never thought of a future with *anyone* until I met you. Of course we both need time to get our bearings; our worlds have been turned upside down. But I'm in."

"Me, too."

"So let's enjoy what we've got and see where it takes us."

He said something to the same effect when, a few days later, she asked him his thoughts on having kids: "I want you, with or without children."

Needless to say, Joely's notes after time spent with Drew are positive: *I've never felt so secure with another person; He was really listening to me; He fits in so great with my family!* There are moments, however, when fear and doubt creep in, and she writes those feelings down, too. But she notices that they only come up after they're together, once she's alone with her own thoughts. Her own notes demonstrate that she's never had a healthier, more satisfying relationship than the one she's in; it's only her own misgivings that get in the way. For this reason, Joely decided that she was ready to bring Drew with her tonight and introduce him to her people.

"Is this *him*?" a baritone voice says behind them.

Joely and Drew turn to see a gentleman in a teal velvet tuxedo and black, square-framed glasses. Joely smiles and kisses him on the cheek. "Yes, Mitchell, this is Drew," she says.

"I didn't know what to expect," Mitchell says, looking Drew up and down. "Now I get it."

They laugh as Drew shakes Mitchell's hand. "Thanks for the compliment, but I doubt I could pull off a suit as sharp as yours."

"That is the correct answer," Mitchell replies, linking his arm through Drew's. "Let's introduce you to everyone."

For the next three hours, Joely watches as Drew proceeds to charm half the room, most of whom are longtime friends of Joely's. While there are more than a few surprised expressions when Joely introduces him as her "boyfriend," the reviews are mostly glowing: "He's fabulous!"; "What a great guy!"; "You two look amazing together!"

By the end of the night, after the auction and the dancing and the flan and the side-splitting laughter, Joely is happily exhausted. Drew, however, is still going strong. Along with making a host of new friends, he's also run into two former clients and has fallen deep into a conversation with two women who are looking to transport their sheep's milk beauty products up the Eastern Seaboard. Joely approaches and puts a hand on his arm.

"The lady is tired," he says to them apologetically. "But we'll talk over lunch next week?"

The couple nods in agreement.

"Nice job, Joely," one of the women says. "You found a straight guy who actually *listens*."

When she arrives home, Joely goes straight for her journal.

*I'm so happy, I'm almost giddy. I can't believe how easily he fell in with everyone. It was strange for me to introduce him to everyone as my partner, but I realized that other people's reactions are irrelevant. It's my own discomfort that I have to get past. I can't say I'm fully there yet, but I want to be, so I'll know it will happen eventually. Drew is great. I'm happy with him. I've done the math, and, for now, this adds up.*

## CHAPTER EIGHT TIP

# P + V = C: How do you add up?

### PERSONALITY

For this variable, use the Big Five personality traits, which are the standards of research psychologists:

Openness

Conscientiousness

Agreeableness

Extroversion

Neuroticism

Rate yourself from 1 to 10 in each of these categories, where 1 = not open at all and 10 = very open, then rate your partner. How aligned are you in each?

### VALUES

This variable is more subjective. List five values that are important to you, such as kindness, open-mindedness, responsibility, family-oriented, fun, or any other traits that you regard highly. Write them down.

Rate yourself from 1 to 10 in each of these categories, then rate your partner. How aligned are you in each?

If you have at least six of the traits that are most important to you in decent alignment, you have a baseline of compatibility, which means the relationship is worth pursuing and exploring. If that alignment increases over time, this is a great sign. If alignment decreases, it may be time to move on.

CHAPTER NINE

# Don't Ignore Red Flags

Part of my job as a dating coach is giving my clients a reality check, for better or worse. This might mean convincing them to date 'em 'til you hate 'em so that they don't miss out on something special. But it can also mean helping them identify potentially destructive, toxic, or damaging behaviors they might be seeing in their partner.

This is not always a simple process. Sometimes, people have their own histories that make it difficult for them to see when something is harmful. Or, they may be so invested in the relationship (or the dream that their partner will change) that it seems impossible to let go. Other times, the situation itself is not easy to classify as black or white, good or bad. Each person has to look inward and see what's right and true for them.

However, there are certain patterns, which I call black flags, that are unacceptable in any form—namely, physical violence and abuse. In the US, one in four women and one in nine men experience severe physical violence from their intimate partner, according to the National Coalition Against Domestic Violence. In addition, reports the Violence Policy Center, three women are killed by an intimate partner every day. If you are in a physically abusive relationship and aren't sure if you should stay, I strongly urge you to consider making a plan to leave. I know this can be difficult, especially if you have a long history or family ties with your partner. But this may be a matter of life and death. (For more resources and information, please consult the list I've compiled in the back of this book.)

Black flags aside, there are three other kinds of signals—red flags, yellow flags, and green lights—that can act as guideposts in your relationship, telling you whether you should move forward or pull back.

Let's break them down.

## Red Flags

When Evan, a thirty-six-year-old medical illustrator, sees Chloe's picture on a dating app, he's intrigued. Okay, more than intrigued. It's rare to find someone in the Washington, DC, area with the same interests as him, who also happens to be beautiful.

A thirty-four-year-old gym manager, Chloe describes herself as an "adrenaline junkie" whose Instagram features "fitspo" posts of her working out and cooking healthy food, as well as pics of her skydiving and bungee jumping. Evan, who plans on going to China this summer to bungee jump off the Zhangjiajie Glass Bridge, can't swipe right fast enough.

On their first date, they meet for coffee at a cute place in Dupont Circle. Evan is bowled over when Chloe arrives, wearing a pair of strategically ripped jeans, a pristine white T-shirt, and a black leather jacket. Her hair, shiny chestnut with blonde highlights, falls lushly past her shoulders. Chloe's makeup is expertly applied, with winged eyeliner and plumped, glossy lips straight out of a TikTok tutorial. If a photographer happened to pop up from behind the counter, she would be ready.

"Nice shoes," he says, pointing to her bright yellow Brooks sneakers. "They're the best for running."

"Agree. And they're super easy to find in my closet."

"I assume that means your closet is . . . um . . . busy?"

"You could say that," she says with a smile. "I might rent the apartment next door to mine just for the extra storage."

Evan almost laughs, then realizes she's serious.

"And," she continues, "I'll have a bigger space to make my workout videos."

"Smart. If you use the place for work, you could probably write it off on taxes."

Her face brightens. "That's what I thought! Great minds . . ."

Over the next hour, Evan learns all about Chloe's work, her family, her likes and dislikes, and even what she wants to name her dog (when she has the time for one). It doesn't occur to him that she doesn't ask him much about himself; she's so entrancing, he could listen to her all day.

A few nights later, Evan and Chloe go hatchet throwing. Chloe is stronger than her petite frame would suggest, but she manages to look perfect even when she's grunting with exertion. When her hatchet lands a couple of centimeters from the bulls-eye, she smiles with satisfaction. "Tough break, man," she teases.

"Didn't anyone ever tell you about counting chickens?" he teases back.

"I think I'm safe to count them."

Evan throws his hatchet—and it hits dead center.

"YES!" He clucks like a chicken and laughs.

"No way!" she says, with a slight bite to her voice. "No. Way."

Evan notices the quick shift in her mood and quickly tries to shift it back. "No big deal," he says, pulling the hatchets out of the target. "You'll probably beat me next time."

Luckily, she does. By the end of the evening, Chloe is all smiles again, and she even gives Evan a kiss goodnight.

Over the next few weeks, Evan and Chloe spend more and more time together, running and working out, going to the movies and out to dinner. Chloe texts and calls Evan often with little messages telling him how fabulous he is, how much she likes him, how happy she is that they found each other. It makes him feel like a million bucks.

Which is why he's surprised by a comment she makes after their date at the Trapeze School, as Evan swaps out his sweaty T-shirt for a flannel shirt.

"I was thinking," Chloe says, "maybe we should get you some new shirts."

"How come? I have plenty of shirts."

"Right, but they're all grungy. It makes you look like a college kid."

Evan's thrown by her criticism, even though she's smiling. "I'm pretty comfortable with what I wear," he says. "I dress professionally at work. This is how I feel relaxed and comfortable."

"Okay," she says, looking out the window. "If that's how you want to look."

A few weeks later, Evan comes out of the shower to find Chloe looking through his texts. He's not sure what bothers him more: what she's doing or the fact that she doesn't seem at all concerned that she's been discovered.

"What are you doing?" he says, trying to keep his voice calm. Maybe there's a good explanation for this.

"Who's Danielle?" Chloe says.

"My coworker."

"Why does she want to meet with you tomorrow?"

"Umm . . . probably because we're short-staffed this week?"

"You sure that's the only reason?"

"Chlo, this feels weird. Are you accusing me of something?"

"I don't know. Should I be?"

"What? No," he says. "Danielle's my *coworker*. That's it."

197

"Hmmm . . ." Chloe says, continuing to scroll.

"I don't really feel comfortable with you looking through my phone," he says.

"The only reason you would feel uncomfortable is if you had something to hide."

She says it so casually that for a moment Evan considers her point. Maybe he's making a big deal out of this.

"I don't have anything to hide," he says. "But I would appreciate it if you would ask me permission before looking at my texts."

"Okay, fine." Chloe tosses the phone toward the foot of the bed. "You don't be so touchy about it."

He heads back into the bathroom feeling disoriented. He wasn't being oversensitive . . . was he? It was a proportionate response . . . right?

Why does he feel like the bad guy here?

From then on, everything Chloe says seems to have an edge to it. Her compliments are backhanded: "I've never seen anyone who can pull off thinning hair like you do"; "Your social media makes you seem so smart"; or, when he takes her out to dinner on her birthday, "I didn't know you could afford such a nice restaurant."

"That's kind of hurtful," he replies.

"What do you mean? I'm saying you picked a great place."

"You said you didn't think I could afford it."

"I just meant that I'm sure it's expensive."

"And that I can't pay for it."

She rolls her eyes. "Oh, my *gosh*, Evan. I can't even give you a *compliment*."

Variations on that theme: *Don't be so sensitive, Don't take everything so personally,* return over and over again. Chloe will do or say something that upsets Evan, but when he tries to express his feelings, she blames him. Evan's frustration builds and he begins to feel distant from her.

"Maybe we should see a therapist," he says after one of their spats.

Her response is swift and decisive: "I'm not going to a therapist just because you can't handle a little criticism."

At a friend's wedding, Evan runs into Jamie, an old friend from college, and spends a few minutes catching up with her before bringing her over to meet Chloe, who has been waiting for him at their table.

"Oh, wow! Hi, Chloe! It's so nice to meet you," says Jamie. "You found yourself a great guy."

Chloe gives her a cool smile. "If you say so."

Jamie picks up on Chloe's dark energy and excuses herself. "It was great to see you, Evan. Nice to meet you, Chloe."

As Jamie walks off, Evan turns to Chloe. "What the heck was that?"

"What was what?"

"You could not have been ruder to her."

"Maybe *she* was rude, chatting up my boyfriend while I sat here by myself."

"Chloe, she was a friend from college. We haven't seen each other in fifteen years."

"Well, you made up for lost time!" she says loudly, causing a few people to turn and look at them.

Evan feels his face turn hot with embarrassment and, inexplicably, guilt. "I'm sorry," he says. "I thought it would be okay to take a few minutes to chat."

"Just like you thought it would be okay to drag me to this wedding, where I know no one, and just . . . abandon me!"

"What do you mean? We were together the entire cocktail hour, we sat together at the ceremony, and we just slow danced for ten minutes."

"And then you left me to go talk to another woman!"

"A *friend*, Chloe. A friend."

"You know what?" Chloe says, rising from her chair. "Why don't you enjoy your evening with your *friends*? Clearly you don't even want me here."

"Of course I do!" In a last-ditch effort to calm things down, Evan reaches for her hand. "I'm thrilled that you're here."

"Nice of you to say that now," she says, still pouting.

"I mean it. You're the most gorgeous woman in the room. I don't know how I got so lucky."

She smiles at him, then gives him a kiss on the end of his nose. "Me neither."

Evan's not sure what makes him more uneasy: how unashamedly Chloe manipulated him, or how easily he allowed her to do it.

The next morning, Evan calls me. He tells me all about Chloe, how they met, the progression of their relationship, all the way up to the previous evening.

"I really care for her, but more and more I feel really off balance," Evan admits. "On the one hand, I feel like she's being unfair, but then I think, maybe I'm the problem. I don't really know how to make this work."

"Maybe you're not supposed to make it work," I say.

"What do you mean? Aren't you all about 'date 'em 'til you hate 'em'?"

"Not when there are so many red flags."

"Red flag" is a term that gets thrown around a lot these days, but it's not one I use lightly. In my book, a red flag is a characteristic or behavioral pattern that is conventionally considered problematic, and makes a satisfying and even safe relationship impossible. In other words, a red flag is a serious, unfixable dealbreaker. And they should never be ignored.

What's tricky about red flags is that they can masquerade as flaws. For example, you may have someone "argumentative" who appreciates a good debate. This may not mean trouble; in fact, some people are energized by fiery discourse. But when it tips over into verbal aggression or yelling, it enters red flag territory. This can be confusing and unclear, depending on your tolerance level. If I grew up in a tense home, an argumentative person may not throw me as much as someone who is used to quiet, thoughtful dialogue. It's still a red flag; it's just harder for some people to see it.

Then again, what one person considers a red flag might be completely acceptable to someone else. I know one man, for example, who was thousands of dollars in debt and had no stable living. For many people, this would be a *huge* red flag. However, he fell in love with a woman who was independently wealthy and had no problem with his financial issues; she even paid off his debts for him. Today they are happily married and she supports them both. When I tell people about this couple, they often respond with outrage: *"How could she let this guy take advantage of her?!?"* The man's finances are a 100 percent, deal-breaking red flag—for *them*. But for his wife, it's no problem. If it doesn't cause harm and both people are happy, it doesn't have to be a red flag.

Even universal red flags, like cheating, don't have to mean the end of a relationship. One couple I know chose to stay together after an infidelity. They saw that one lapse as a sign of deeper trouble and went to therapy to work it out. Many years have passed since then and they are still happily married. However, they were only successful because it was a one-time lapse by someone who was immediately willing to make a change. Had this person been a regular cheater who did nothing to fix the problem, it's unlikely that this couple would still be together. In these instances, it's not a question of whether or not the behavior is problematic—it absolutely is—but whether or not the person chooses to do something about it.

Certain red flags, however, such as manipulation and cruelty, are always deal-breakers, no matter how you slice them. And this is what I see in Chloe.

I'm not a therapist, but if I had to classify Chloe's patterns, I'd say they very closely resemble narcissism, a personality type that is excessively self-centered, often at the expense of others. These are people who are predominantly concerned with their wants, needs, and experience, to the point where they are unable to feel empathy for other people. In fact, narcissists have little genuine concern for those around them; they just manipulate others to meet their own desires and ambitions and affirm their own importance. This is exactly what Chloe is doing with Evan. In the beginning, she love-bombed him with sweet notes and calls, drawing him in. Then came the cruel, backhanded comments, a classic narcissist move to dominate and control others by undermining their confidence. She steamrolled Evan's boundaries by looking at his phone without permission, and when he spoke up about it, Chloe gaslit him, turning the behavior around to make Evan question his own judgment. Finally, Chloe threw a tantrum at the wedding because she wasn't the center of Evan's (and maybe even everyone else's) attention. This is a person who is only concerned with herself, her appearance, and other people's perception of her. She is not interested in giving, only taking, which makes a true relationship with her impossible.

"But she's not always like that," Evan argues. "Sometimes, she's really great."

"I'm sure she is, which is probably what makes her behavior so difficult and painful to deal with."

"But what if I talked to her about it? Can't people change their behavior?"

This question has kept more people than I can count in red-flag relationships. They dream that their partner will transform into some new, improved version of themselves and all will be well. To be fair, there are some outliers who do it. They recognize a problem and are motivated to change. But most people don't.

Ultimately, it comes down to patterns. Did they only behave this way once or twice, or is it a running theme? We're all guilty of losing our temper or acting out once in a while. But if a damaging behavior is recurring and consistent, it's a real red flag.

"Considering that Chloe refused to go to therapy, I doubt she sees any need to change," I say. "So you have to assume things are going to stay exactly the way they are. Is that a situation you can live with? Could you be happy, long-term, with someone who treats you the way Chloe does? Would you allow anyone to treat someone you love like that?"

"I understand what you're saying," Evan replies. "But it's hard for me to see things in such black-and-white terms. It's true, Chloe can be really difficult, but when it's good, it's *really* good. Maybe it's not as bad as I'm making it out to be."

Evan's in a tough position, because those sticky-sweet moments he's describing are the glue that's keeping him trapped in the spider's web. It's not easy to walk away from a good thing that, in reality, isn't that good. Lots of people need support in order to do it. (In fact, many seek the help of a professional therapist.) But, in every case, it doesn't happen until they really see the truth for themselves.

"Maybe it's not," I concede, "but only you can decide that. My suggestion is to take a week and watch the patterns. After each conversation and date, write down the behaviors you see and how you feel. Then evaluate the ratio between the 'good' and 'difficult'. Is the tradeoff worth it?"

Over the next week, Evan records his observations on paper, which helps him separate his emotion from the facts. And the facts don't lie: some of the time, being with Chloe is wonderful. But a lot of the time, she's hurtful, dismissive, and manipulative. In fact, Evan notes, he has said "I'm sorry" twenty-three times over that week, even though he hasn't actually done anything wrong.

"I hate to say this," he admits to me, "but I'm unhappy more than I'm happy with Chloe. I think her behavior is a deal-breaker."

"I'm sorry, Evan, but I'm also not sorry. I'm glad you listened to your instincts and recognize this red flag for what it is. Now you can move on to someone who will treat you with respect and decency."

## Yellow Flags

When Adam walks into Olivia's coffee shop and bakery, Flour Power, and orders a coffee butterscotch muffin, Olivia barely gives him a second glance; during the morning rush, she can't think of anything beyond the next order. But about twenty minutes later, after the crowd thins, he returns to the counter. "I just wanted to tell you how much I loved the muffin," he says. "Is that a new flavor?"

Adam's gorgeous smile snaps Olivia to attention like a hit of espresso.

"Yeah, it is," she says, smiling back. "I'm test-driving some new recipes."

"Well, this one passes with all the horsepower . . . or whatever."
He blushes. "Sorry, I was trying for a pun there . . ."

She laughs, melting a little at his sweet awkwardness. "I got
what you were going for. Looks like this recipe's staying in rotation."

"Good move. I'm Adam."

"Olivia."

"Nice to meet you. I guess now I know the muffin man. Woman."
Olivia bursts out laughing. "*That* was terrible."

Adam laughs, too. "Made you smile, though, which was what
I was going for."

Over the next half hour, as cinnamon-sugar rugelach bake in
the oven, Olivia learns that Adam is a twenty-eight-year-old dog
trainer and a lifelong resident of Portland, Oregon. He loves his
grandmother, the Portland Pickles, and has three bulldogs named
Alvin, Simon, and Theodore. Their chat is fun and breezy, albeit
interrupted at intervals by the orders of morning regulars, the
hiss of the coffee machine . . . and Adam's phone.

"I'm so sorry," he says, when it pings for the third time in as
many minutes. "I just have to answer this DM. I started posting
training videos on Instagram and now I'm getting all these client
requests . . ."

He taps at the phone for a long minute, then looks up at Olivia
and blinks, as if recalling she was there. "Sorry about that. Listen,
I can see you're busy. I really came over to ask if you wanted to go
out sometime."

"You mean, you were just using the muffin as an opener?"
Olivia says.

"Maybe," he admits with a laugh, "but I wasn't lying. It was really good."

Adam walks out of Flour Power with Olivia's number and plans to meet the next night for dinner and craft beers at a brewery near Washington Park. Olivia, meanwhile, floats light as air through the rest of the day, like a perfect soufflé.

The next night, Olivia arrives at McKellar's five minutes early, as per her habit; as a baker, she operates by the clock. Sliding into a booth, Olivia tells the server she'll hold off on ordering a drink until her date gets here.

"Shouldn't be more than a couple of minutes," she assures him.

A couple of minutes turns out to be fifteen. When Adam arrives, all smiles, he doesn't seem the least bit concerned about it. "8:45 on the button," he jokes. "Only five minutes late."

"I thought we said 8:30."

"Well, I was always taught that there's a ten-minute window in which you're still considered 'on time.' So, technically . . ."

"Interesting," Olivia replies. "I was always taught, 'If you're early, you're on time. If you're on time, you're late. And if you're late, you're fired.'"

Adam laughs. "I guess it's good you're your own boss."

"Just means I'm always the first one at the bakery. 4:50 a.m. on the dot."

"Whoa. How are you awake right now?"

"Coffee. Probably nerves, too," she admits.

He grins at her. "So I'm not the only one."

The rest of the date goes off without a hitch, though Olivia does notice that Adam's phone gets its own seat of honor next to his plate. Every time it lights up, his eyes dart to it. Sometimes, they flit right back to Olivia. Other times, he'll respond to something, then return to the conversation. Olivia finds it distracting, especially when it throws off the flow of the conversation and she has to remind him what they were talking about. But when he's engaged, she enjoys herself immensely—enough so that, when he asks her out again, she happily says yes.

That date, however, never happens. After Olivia takes a post-work power nap, does her hair and makeup, and slides into the car to drive to her date, she gets a text from Adam: *Can't make it tonight. So sorry. I'll call to reschedule.*

Now Olivia's annoyed. Having to cancel is one thing, but doing so twenty minutes before the date is something else entirely.

*I wish you'd told me earlier,* she replies. *It's good you caught me before I left the house.*

*So sorry. Can I make it up to you?*

He follows this with a picture of his three dogs with pleading looks in their eyes.

Though she's still irritated, she can't help but laugh. She reminds herself that not everyone is as time-obsessed as she is; even her employees have teased her about it. And at least Adam apologized. At least he didn't stand her up.

*Sure,* Olivia writes. *But only if the dogs come.*

Adam keeps to his word and brings Alvin, Simon, and Theodore to meet Olivia outside the bakery after closing time.

They bombard her with kisses and snuggles, winding themselves and their leashes around her legs so enthusiastically that she has to sit down on the sidewalk, laughing, and untangle herself.

"You'd never know from these guys that I am, in fact, a dog trainer," Adam says, helping her out.

"It's probably because I'm covered with sugar."

"Good point. I blame you."

Olivia laughs again.

After a substantial cuddle-fest, Olivia runs up to her apartment above the bakery to shower and change, and then they head out for dinner at Aufessen, a German deli with sandwiches stuffed a foot thick with cured salami and tubs of sauerkraut. Sitting at outdoor picnic tables, Adam and Olivia compete to see who can open their jaws wider to fit the entire sandwich, laughing so hard they can barely take a bite. They laugh even harder when Alvin eats a piece of salami that falls off Olivia's plate and his eyes go wide when he realizes how spicy it is.

After dinner, they walk off the food and talk about the pressures of running your own business. "Most twenty-nine-year-olds don't have the same responsibilities that I do," Olivia says. "Not just the expenses for the business, but also other people's livelihoods. If the bakery goes under, my employees will lose their jobs."

"I don't think you have to worry about that," Adam says. "Your place is amazing. There's a line out the door every morning. Whatever you're doing, you're doing it right."

It's not until he says it that Olivia realizes how much she needed to hear it. "Thank you, Adam. I really appreciate that."

As Adam opens the door to his car, he says, "Oh, man. I left my phone in here. I guess I forgot it when I took the dogs out of the car."

"It missed a great date," says Olivia.

"Agree. So, when's the next one?"

Three days later, Olivia arrives at a park under St. Joseph's Bridge, where a small concert is underway. On the grass, people sit on blankets and beach chairs while a bluegrass band plays their hearts out. Olivia unrolls a blanket of her own and sets a picnic basket on it. Then she checks her phone.

Adam is already five minutes late.

Olivia tells herself to relax and enjoy the music, which she attempts to do while keeping an eye out for a sign of Adam. Thirty minutes go by, and she decides she's had enough. She packs up the basket, her blanket, puts on her cardigan and heads back toward her car—just as Adam appears.

"I know, I know," he says with a smile. "I'm fired."

"You said it, I didn't," Olivia replies tartly, walking past him.

"Wait, wait. You're leaving?"

"Yeah, I'm leaving."

"Why?"

"Because I'm tired of waiting for you."

"But I'm here now!"

"I don't just mean *now*," she says. "I'm tired of waiting for you in general. Correction: I'm tired of being left waiting."

"I'm sorry, Olivia. I just had this call I couldn't—"

"I get it. Your phone takes priority. Your time is more important than mine."

"It's not like that."

"Well, showing up late on the regular and being stuck to your
phone the entire time says otherwise."

"Look," says Adam. "I'm sorry."

"Me, too."

"Come on. We can't just call a do-over?"

She looks at him sadly and shakes her head. "Not today."

As Olivia drives away, it takes everything in her not to look in
the rearview mirror, where Adam's reflection is getting smaller
and smaller.

"I think I should break up with him," Olivia tells me later that day.

"Possibly," I say, "but let's not make a full stop just yet. You're
dealing with a yellow flag, not a red one, so let's just slow down
and evaluate."

Yellow flags are qualities that give someone pause, like the
"bothers" we spoke about in Chapter Six; they may not sound
an alarm like red flags do, but they shouldn't be ignored, either.
Sometimes, a yellow flag can turn into a red flag based on the
degree to which it triggers a person. For example, owning a pet
snake isn't a red flag, but it can be a bright yellow for someone
with a fear of reptiles. Some yellow flags, like an unkempt beard,
are small, fixable annoyances that make little difference to the
relationship as a whole.

"Tell me the things that are really bothering you about Adam," I continue.

"I hate that he's late all the time. That he's inconsistent. That he's constantly checking his phone."

"How does it make you feel when he does that?"

"Vulnerable. Like I'm more invested than he is. Like he doesn't care about me or my time."

"Do you think that's true?"

"No. I think he really does like me."

"And you feel the same?"

"Yeah. I see a lot of potential with Adam—when he's engaged with me."

"Okay," I say. "So have you talked to him about how his lateness and inconsistency affect you?"

"I sort of hinted before, and then today, when I was angry, I said I was tired of waiting for him."

"But you haven't sat down and had a real conversation about it?"

"No, I guess not."

"Then that's your next step. Give him a call and explain why you were angry. Tell him how it makes you feel when he shows up late, cancels at the last minute, or pays more attention to his phone than to you. Then see how he responds. If he's willing to make some changes, you've got something to work with. If not, then you have your answer."

So that's what Olivia does. And to her surprise and delight, the conversation goes very well. Adam is attentive, responsive, and even apologizes for hurting her feelings. From now on, he commits to putting his phone on silent and leaving it in his pocket when he's out with her. However, he asks her for patience when it comes to his issues with time management. "It's something I've struggled with for a long time," he says. "I'll try to do better to be on time for our dates, and I'll be in touch earlier if I have to cancel. But I'm probably not going to do it perfectly."

The fact that Adam is honest about his shortcomings but willing to work on them encourages Olivia to be more flexible about her standards of timeliness and consistency. And so the yellow flag mellows from a point of contention into a launchpad for both of them to grow.

## Green Lights

Alyson is the consummate introvert, as evidenced by the coffee mug her brother gave her for her birthday: "Want to be invited. Don't want to come."

It's not that Alyson doesn't have friends, but she's shy and reserved by nature. In her twenties and early thirties, she let her friends drag her to all the bars, clubs, and restaurants in her native New Orleans, in hopes of finding her partner. While her friends danced and flirted, Alyson gravitated to the perimeter of the room. It took her days to recover from the forced social-ization, which, as time passed, seemed more and more counter-productive. Online dating was slightly more fruitful; she met the two men with whom she had serious relationships online—though both had ended disappointingly. They were frustrated by Alyson's shyness, mistaking it for coldness or lack of investment, and they were impatient with how long it took for her to come out of her shell. But the harder they pushed, the more closed she got, until the connection dried up and died. Now, at thirty-nine, Alyson is tired: tired of looking, tired of trying, tired of failing. In her view, her time is better spent in the comfort of her house and in the company of Mambo, a three-legged cat she found outside a Chinese restaurant.

So she's completely uninterested when Cory, Alyson's "work wife" from her last job, wants to set her up with Greg, a widower who Cory has known for years.

Alyson's heart goes out to him, but . . . a *widower*? Does she really want to compete with a first, likely beloved, wife?

"I know what you're thinking, but you're just going to have to trust me on this one," Cory continues. "I saw him the other day and I just *knew* it. He's the good man you deserve."

A few nights later, Alyson alights from the streetcar onto Magazine Street, where she finds Greg waiting for her in front of a brightly lit bistro.

And he is *something.*

Alyson takes in his dark skin, thick, black hair, light eyes, and the dimples that form in his cheeks when he smiles. There's something comforting about the gentle way he shakes her hand and the sound of his voice, warm and smooth as honey.

"Cory has only the best things to say about you," Greg says.

"She's fantastic," Alyson says.

"Takes one to know one." Greg pulls open the door to the restaurant, gesturing for her to enter. "Shall we?"

Alyson nods and heads inside, feeling Greg right behind her, his hand subtly shadowing the small of her back. At their table, Greg pulls out her chair.

Alyson cannot remember the last time—if there ever *was* a time—that a man held open a door for her and pulled out her chair. But she'll take it.

Over dinner, they talk about where they're from—while she's NOLA born and bred, he grew up in Lafayette, about two hours away, with his parents, siblings, and his grandmother, who was a stickler for gentility and manners. "She was strict, but she was also loving. And *funny*. People didn't know that about her. She was shy with people she didn't know well, so they thought she was serious, even a snob."

Alyson smiles. "I get that."

"Why? Are you shy?"

"Well, I had one date call me 'the Sphinx.'"

"Ouch. I hope you didn't go out with him again."

"I didn't. It's not easy out there for the shy ones. A lot of people don't have the patience to find out what we have to say."

"Well, a lot of people are missing out. The longer you wait for something, the more you appreciate it when you get it."

Greg smiles at her, and it feels like a door in her heart swings open.

On their next date, they head to the French Quarter, just waking up on this early Sunday afternoon. They pick up coffee and beignets at Cafe du Monde, where Alyson notes how gracious Greg is with the service staff ("Thanks for the extra milk.

215

I really appreciate it") and the generous tip he leaves in the jar. As they walk through the nearby park, Alyson notes how relaxed she feels talking to him, probably because it's her cues that are steering the conversation. Greg listens intently when she talks, asking her about her work (she's close to finishing a major, year-and-a-half-long project) and her favorite books (*One Hundred Years of Solitude* is an all-time favorite). However, when he asks Alyson about her past relationships, she says, "There's not much to tell."

"Is that the case, or do you just not want to talk about it?"

"Not today."

"Cool," Greg replies. "Have you been to the Sculpture Garden Behind NOMA?"

*Whoa*, she thinks. *That was easy*. Never before has a date simply respected her boundaries, not taken her reticence personally, and moved on with such ease.

A few weeks later, just as Alyson sends in the final edit of the manuscript she's slaved over for eighteen months, her phone rings. It's Greg.

"What are you up to?"

"I just finished."

"What? The project?"

"Yeah. Just now."

"That's incredible! Oh, my gosh! Hold on . . . I'll call you right back."

Five minutes later, Alyson's phone rings again.

216

"Get dressed. Something nice," Greg says. "We're going out to celebrate."

Three hours later, they're enjoying a gorgeous Cajun-Creole dinner at Lagniappe, laughing over cocktails and Bananas Foster. As their server clears away dessert, Alyson says, "You ever finish a meal and feel sad? Like you're saying goodbye to a friend?"

Greg laughs. "I have something for you."

He pulls a gift bag from underneath the table and places it in front of her. Alyson smiles at him, then digs through the tissue paper to pull out a hardcover copy of *One Hundred Years of Solitude*. On the cover page is an inscription: *Con gratitud, Gabriel García Márquez.*

"Wait . . ." Alyson says, dumbfounded. "Is this . . . ?"

"First edition in English, signed by the author," Greg replies.

"I can't believe this!"

"There's a card, too," he says shyly.

Alyson reaches back into the bag to find the small card, which reads:

> Dear Alyson,
> I read online that Márquez had to sell his car so his
> family had something to live on while he wrote. It took
> him eighteen months and a lot of perseverance to finish,
> but he did it. And so did you.
> I'm proud of you.
>
> > Fondly,
> > Greg

That's when Alyson realizes: Cory hadn't given this man half the credit he deserves.

"Lucky you," I tell Alyson. "This man is a highway of green lights."

These green lights are qualities that indicate that Greg is a high-quality human: holding the door and pulling out her chair, treating people (particularly service people) with courtesy and respect, showing appreciation, listening to Alyson and honoring her boundaries, celebrating her successes, and going out of his way to give her a gift he knows she'll appreciate. Greg's actions demonstrate that he's a good person and also knows how to be a good partner.

Some green lights, like the ones above, are easy to identify because they are universally accepted as good qualities. But other green lights are specific to each person. For example, Alyson is someone who needs space, and Greg is more than willing to give it. For someone else, that emotional distance might feel like abandonment. Neither perspective is better or worse; it's simply what's right for you. As long as a quality sparks you in a good and healthy way, you can consider it a green light.

Of course, a profusion of green lights doesn't mean that a relationship is absolutely perfect, because no relationship is. As we saw at the beginning, the fact that Greg is a widower was an initial yellow flag for Alyson, but the degree of yellow (manageable) and its ratio to green (low) means that it doesn't have to be an obstruction to the relationship. At the core, Alyson likes Greg,

Greg likes Alyson, both are good partners, so they're both willing to accept the "stuff" they bring to the table.

It's unrealistic to think a relationship will be all green lights all the time. In fact, I advise my clients to make a list of five strengths and five weaknesses in the person they're dating. If they can only see the great stuff, they're in an "artificial green" zone. It's not a real relationship; they're just infatuated. In a "real green" relationship, you have a clear and balanced view of the other person. You know their gifts and challenges, but to you, the whole package is sweet.

## CHAPTER NINE TIP

## Green Lights

Green lights are positive traits or qualities that attract you to your partner and indicate that a healthy relationship with them is likely.

### EXAMPLES

1. Pursues you genuinely, without pressure.
2. Gives the relationship proper attention and time to develop.
3. Shows active interest in you by asking questions about your character, preferences, and interests.
4. Acts in ways you respect.
5. Treats you with courtesy and respects your boundaries.

## Yellow Flags

Yellow flags are traits or qualities that give you pause or that you don't appreciate, but do not necessarily spell the end of the relationship.

### EXAMPLES

1. Inconsiderate or unwilling to accommodate. (Have you had four+ dates and you always had to be the one to travel?)
2. Not present or available. (Do you have to hunt down the other person for a date or phone conversation?)
3. Does not show adequate investment in the relationship. (Are you feeling like you may be the only one interested?)
4. Unreliable or inconsistent. (Has your date let you down or canceled at the last minute without explanation?)
5. Does not spark your interest. (Are you constantly checking your watch on dates?)

Examine yellow flags closely and ask yourself if they are something you can live with for the long term. What effect will this behavior have on your life? Is it simply annoying or something deeper?

# Red Flags

Red flags are danger signs. They are more than a characteristic you don't like; they are indicators that a healthy relationship is impossible.

## EXAMPLES

1. Jealous or possessive.
2. Controlling.
3. Manipulative.
4. Interested in your money/social status.
5. Critical of you, those close to you, and things you care about.
6. Violate your personal boundaries and/or your privacy.
7. Disrespect, blame, shame, put you down, and find fault.
8. Gaslight you and/or blame you for their bad behavior.
9. Quick to anger.
10. Profess their deep feelings or "love bomb" quickly into the relationship.
11. Unable to show compassion and empathy.
12. Dishonest.
13. Pressure you to do what's important to them, even at the cost of what's important to you.
14. Make you feel emotionally and physically unsafe, or show signs of emotional of physical abuse.

It can be hard to differentiate a flaw from a red flag, so watch carefully. While some things may improve over time, rudeness or disrespect are traits you probably don't want in a life partner and possible future co-parent. Listen to your instincts and rely on mentors and good friends who will tell you the truth.

The longer a relationship lasts, the harder it is to get out of it. When there is a red flag, gather your information, make a decision, and take action as quickly as you can.

# CHAPTER TEN

# Convince Me Why You're Breaking Up

S o you've given it your all with the person you're dating, but no dice. You've decided it's time to break up.

Not so fast.

If you want to end the relationship, you're going to have to convince me first—and not because I'm trying to get you to stay with Mr. or Ms. Not-So-Perfect. Quite the contrary. It's because, if you're really going to call it quits, you need to be 100 percent certain that it's the right decision. Otherwise, you might end up re-dating this person five years down the line to get an answer you could have gotten today. Why waste your precious time?

A good argument for breaking up begins with a solid *why*. Like any good lawyer, you'll need a clear case and the confidence to back it up. If you're really convinced, selling me should be a breeze.

But don't think I'm going down quietly; I am a professional devil's advocate. My job is to provide the opposing force that will either strengthen or break your argument. It might drive you crazy in the moment, but I promise you'll thank me later.

Just ask a few of my clients.

## Claire and Jack

In the Dance Break studio in Williamsburg, Brooklyn, Claire leads twelve fourth-graders in their barre exercises. Just as she guides them into fifth position, a man barrels through the door, all energy in his ripped jeans and Guns n' Roses T-shirt. He freezes as the music stops and everyone in the room turns to stare at him.

"Hi!" he booms. "I'm supposed to pick up Elias?"

"Hi, Uncle Jack!" comes a voice toward the end of the barre. It belongs to a sweet-faced boy who waves excitedly.

The man waves back. "Oh, hey, buddy!"

"We don't end until 4:45," says Claire in a calm, quiet voice.

"Oh, man, I'm so sorry. I must have gotten the time mixed up."

"That's okay. If you want, you can take a seat on one of those beanbag chairs by the piano." Claire gestures to a corner of the room, where a cluster of adult-sized beanbags are arranged in a semicircle. One is occupied by a mother working on her laptop and another by a teenage boy wearing headphones and scrolling on his phone.

"Great," Jack replies, quietly creeping across the wood floor. Claire, with slow, fluid movements, cues the dancers again, but before they can tendu, a loud BANG makes everyone in the room jump: Jack, underestimating how low the beanbag was, loses his balance and hits the floor, hard. Even the kid with the headphones is startled.

For a tense moment, everyone stares at Jack, who laughs and says, "I missed."

The students titter, and even Claire can't help but crack a smile.

"Are you okay?" she asks.

"My behind will be fine," Jack groans, sliding onto the beanbag. "My ego, not so much."

Claire gives him a sympathetic look, then shifts her focus back to the kids. As she leads them through their barre exercises and small jumps, she occasionally catches Jack's reflection in the mirror. Each time, he's looking directly at her—or giving a thumbs-up to Elias. This guy isn't at all her type; with a tall, lanky frame, too-long hair, and dire need for a shave, he looks nothing like the big, clean-cut men she's always dated. He's also constantly in motion, tapping his foot, drumming his hands on his knees. But she has to admit he's charming.

After class, as the students pirouette out of the room, Jack approaches Claire with Elias at his side. "I just wanted to apologize for interrupting. I know it's not easy to keep kids' attention, even without some dude making a commotion."

"No problem," Claire says.

"I also wanted to know if I could take you out sometime?"

Claire's expression switches from gracious to surprised. Though she half-expected the question, she didn't think he would ask it in front of his nephew. Her eyes fall on Elias, who is smiling hopefully at her. "Uncle Jack's really nice, Miss Claire. I think you should say yes."

Claire laughs. "Well, if Elias says so . . ."

Their first date is at Barcade, a bar stocked with classic, old-school arcade games. It isn't exactly Claire's scene—the noise and lights are a lot for her—but once she gets into Donkey Kong, she has a good time. Jack is funny, gracious, and smart, a great date in every sense. But the attraction factor is neutral at best.

However, as a former client of mine, Claire knows that neutral could still mean potential, so she goes out with him a few more times to see if things shift. And in some ways, they do. Jack is a voracious reader, so the conversations are always interesting. He also takes her to places she's never heard of before, despite living in Brooklyn for over ten years. His perspective is so different from hers, it feels like she's always learning something new just by being around him.

But when it comes to chemistry, she's still hitting a wall. Once again, Claire digs into her "Aleeza" toolbox to try and create it intentionally. She asks Jack lots of questions about himself, seeks out and compliments him on his good points, looks him in the eyes (the windows to the soul), and makes a point of addressing him by name, which creates connection and intimacy. Knowing he's a fan of George Carlin, she even buys him a mug with a quote from the comedian: "Some people have no idea what they're doing and a lot of them are really good at it.".

To some extent, these efforts work. It's crystal clear to Claire that Jack is a fantastic person. But after three months of dating, Claire sits across the table from him at a raw food restaurant in Park Slope, and it hits her: *I just don't know if he's my partner.*

That night, she calls me.

"I think I should break up with Jack."

"Okay," I say. "Give me one good reason."

"I don't feel a spark. I'm not attracted to him at all."

"I assume you've put in some elbow grease in that department?"

"I've done all the things, Aleeza, every trick you've taught me. I even held off on touching for six dates. But it just isn't there."

"Do you like him as a person?"

"Very much. He's a really great guy. Smart, considerate, gracious . . ."

"And that hasn't sold you?"

"I mean, it has, but it's just not . . . I don't know . . ." She groans with exasperation.

It sounds to me like some key element is missing between Claire and Jack that would ideally shift her from liking him as a person to choosing him as her person. But I think Claire is holding out for this to change.

"Claire, are you 100 percent convinced that Jack isn't right for you?"

Claire thinks for a minute. "Almost, but not completely. Maybe 95 percent. Ninety-eight? Ugh, I just really want this to work out because he's such a good guy."

"I completely understand. Maybe you should give it some more time before you decide. Remember: if there's even a shred of doubt about breaking up, it's not time to do it."

"Okay," she says. "I'm going to give this two more dates, and then I'll decide for sure."

So that's what she does. A few days later, Claire and Jack pick up coffee (well, green tea for Claire) and take a walk around the Brooklyn Botanic Garden. As they talk, Claire considers the prospect that this could be their last date. Two emotions pop up in response: relief, because she won't have to keep trying to push an immovable object, and happiness, because Jack really is a great guy and, without her in the way, he'll have a chance to find someone who's excited about him.

And that's how she knows with 100 percent clarity that it's time to end it with him.

Just then, Jack stops walking and exhales nervously. "I have something to say and if I don't say it now I'm going to find a million excuses not to say it."

Claire braces herself for an emotional declaration. *Oh, no. How am I going to get out of this?*

"I think we should stop seeing each other," says Jack.

She's so shocked, her mouth actually falls open.

"I think you're fantastic, really," he continues. "Being around you has been very grounding for me. But I just don't think we have a future together. We're too different."

Claire is speechless, so Jack keeps talking. "I don't want to hurt you, but I thought I should be honest instead of lead—"

"This is great!" she exclaims.

"Huh?"

"I just decided to break up with you, but I was so nervous about hurting your feelings. Then you broke up with me! Thank you!"

Claire hugs him in gratitude and Jack smiles.

"I meant what I said, by the way," says Jack. "You really are great. That's why I put off ending it."

"I was thinking the same thing! You're a fantastic guy, but just . . ."

"Not for you?"

"YES!"

They both laugh.

On her walk home, Claire calls to tell me what happened.

"I've never heard anyone so happy to get dumped," I say. "Safe to say, I'm convinced."

## Karyn and Steve

A lot has changed in Karyn's life in the last three years. On her thirtieth birthday in New York City, she made a wish for the bravery to pursue her dream of being a special effects makeup artist. On her thirty-third birthday in Los Angeles, she's almost finished with her program at the SPFX Makeup School. This year, she doesn't know what to wish for; she's happier than she's ever been.

At least, she thinks she is, until she comes home one day to find a man in a Bruins jersey sitting on her front stoop, reading a magazine.

"Can I help you?" she says.

"Yeah, hi, I'm Steve," he says. "Natalie's brother? I'm just waiting for her to come home. She didn't tell me she had a housemate."

"She doesn't. Natalie's place is next door."

"Are you serious?" Steve chuckles. "I just got in from Providence—I've been sitting here for half an hour!"

"No problem. People confuse our houses all the time. At least once a week, the Amazon guy drops her packages here."

"She ever get anything good?"

"I don't open them!"

"I would. But only Natalie's: big brother privileges and all. I don't go around opening random people's packages."

Karyn laughs. "Sure you don't."

"I don't!" Steve replies, laughing, too.

And so they spend the next forty-five minutes chatting on Karyn's stoop. Steve is funny and down-to-earth, very different from the ambitious, self-involved LA types Karyn usually meets. She learns that he's forty-one, divorced with two kids, and a die-hard hockey fan. When Natalie finally comes home, Karyn is disappointed that the conversation has to end.

"I hope he wasn't bugging you too much," says Natalie apologetically.

Karyn chuckles. "He was alright."

"Just alright?" Steve says, playing wounded. "I thought I was bowling you over with charm."

Natalie rolls her eyes. "Leave her alone, Stevie, and bring your bag over to my place . . ."

As his sister heads inside, Steve turns back to Karyn. "Seriously. Could I take you out while I'm here?"

Karyn smiles in reply.

Over the next week, Karyn and Steve go out four times. They have a great time together, going out to eat, seeing an LA Kings game, and hitting a karaoke bar with Natalie and some of her friends. Almost every evening after Natalie goes to bed (she's a nurse who works early shifts), Steve knocks on Karyn's door and they stay up talking for hours. Neither expected their time together to be more than just two people enjoying each other's company, but by the end of the week it's clear to both that there's something special happening between them.

"I don't want this to end," he tells her before he heads to the airport. "Could we keep it going?"

"We could try. I've never done the long-distance thing before."

"Me neither. But this is the age of technology. Technically, we can still see each other every day."

She laughs. "True. So I guess I'll see you later, then."

"Yep. See you later."

The next few months go as smoothly as possible, considering the obstacles of a bicoastal relationship. Emails and texts shoot back and forth between them, and they try to connect on video at least once every couple of days (though it's not always easy between the time change, her classes, and his kids' schedule). Despite the odds, their connection deepens, especially when Steve flies out to LA again to celebrate Karyn's graduation from her makeup program. It means a lot to her that he wants to be there.

Just a few weeks later, Karyn lands in Providence with incredible news: she's just been hired by one of the best FX studios in the business and is starting work on a Netflix series next week!

"That's amazing!" Steve says with enthusiasm—but, Karyn notes, not with his usual, full gusto.

"You okay?" she asks.

"Yeah, yeah, just exhausted. Danny wanted to talk last night—he has a crush on an eighth-grader—so we were up pretty late."

Karyn appreciates Steve's dedication to his kids. In fact, after hearing so much about them, she feels like she knows them. And now, apparently, she's getting the chance to meet them in person: Steve says he's scheduled a pizza dinner with the kids while she's in Providence.

The prospect excites and terrifies her. On the one hand, she can't wait to meet Steve's kids, who sound fantastic. But on the other, will meeting them set something in motion that she won't be able to stop?

Steve spends the next three days pulling out all the stops for Karyn, showing her around Providence, seeing a Bruins game (of course), taking her on a tour of the mansions in Newport, and even stealing an afternoon on the beach in Cape Cod. Steve also introduces Karyn to some of his friends and extended family, all of whom welcome her warmly.

"You have a great life here," she tells him after a fun dinner out with a couple of Steve's cousins.

Steve beams. "I'm really glad you think so. I've been working really hard to sell you on it."

Karyn reads the subtext: Steve wants *her* to like his life, too. Maybe enough to consider becoming a part of it.

Again she feels that mix of joy and dread. She really, really likes Steve, even more than she did when they first started dating. But enough to move to Providence? Enough to give up her life in LA?

Karyn sleeps poorly that night, her last night with Steve, and is exhausted the next morning. As she nurses a cup of coffee, Steve says he's going to call the kids' mom to confirm a pick-up time.

"Wait," says Karyn.

"What?"

"I don't think you should call her."

"Why not?"

"I don't . . . I don't think I'm ready to meet them."

Steve puts his phone down. "Okay."

"It's not that I don't want to. I really, really do," Karyn says. "But I don't want to confuse anyone."

"What's confusing?"

"Meeting your kids means that you and I are really serious."

"We've been flying across the country to see each other," says Steve. "I'd say that's pretty serious."

"Yes," she concedes, "but it's only been a few months. I don't think either of us really knows where this is going."

"Well," he says, sitting down next to her. "I was hoping this was going toward serious. I really care for you, Karyn. I want to give this a chance."

"I care for you, too, but . . . I don't know if I'm ready for that. I need to think about it."

Steve is quiet for a minute, then says, "Okay. Let me know what you think."

Karyn's thoughts jumble the entire flight home. As soon as she gets into an Uber at LAX, she calls me to help her make sense of them: "Aleeza, I'm absolutely terrified."

"Probably because your head is in the future," I say. "Let's try to bring it back to the present."

Karyn exhales slowly. "Okay."

"First of all, I want to commend you for putting a stop to the outing with his kids," I say. "If you're not completely sure about this, it's better not to involve them."

"Thanks. It didn't feel good to do."

"Telling the truth can be uncomfortable, but it's usually the kindest option. So let's get honest. Where's this fear coming from?"

"I think it's the expectation I felt from Steve. He basically said he was hoping I would fall in love with Providence and want to move there. I'll admit, it's a nice place to live. And I love being with him. But I have a life in LA, a dream career I just started."

"I'm not belittling your career; I know you've worked very hard to get where you are," I say. "But there will always be another job. There won't always be the right partner."

"So I'm supposed to give up everything for him?"

"Would you have to?"

"Maybe not everything, but certainly a lot. My friends, my new job. There's no market for special effects makeup in Rhode Island. The closest I can get is New York, but that's mostly for stage, print, and fashion. I really want to work in film and television; that's why I went to LA. In New York, I'd have to make all new contacts, which would be really hard if I had to commute back and forth to Providence all the time. I'd probably just end up resenting Steve."

Generally, I believe that finding a partner is worth a career pivot, especially early in a career that's not well established yet. But Karyn is insightful enough to realize that certain changes can ask too much of a person and of a relationship. After all, she would be turning her life upside down and Steve would barely have to change anything.

"Do you think there's a possibility that Steve would consider moving to LA?" I ask.

"I don't think so," says Karyn, "and I would never ask him to do that. He loves his kids and it's important to him to be in their everyday lives. They deserve to have their dad as much as possible."

What Karyn is describing here is a major logistical hurdle. She's correct that trying to make a future with Steve at this point would be difficult. But generally, logistics aren't the cause of the kind of fear that Karyn's experiencing. I wonder if there's something deeper going on.

"Karyn," I say, "Do you want kids?"

"Yeah, of course. I've always wanted to be a mom."

"What if you could become a mom tomorrow?"

Karyn laughs. "Oh, my gosh, no. I'm not ready for that. I was thinking maybe five, six years from now, if I find a partner."

And therein lies the problem.

This isn't only about geographics; Karyn's and Steve's timelines are off. Steve is forty-one. He's been married already and has two kids in middle school. He's thinking of the long game: settling down, making a life with someone, maybe having another child or two. Karyn is thirty-three and in no rush to settle down. She wants to build her career and explore the world before committing to a partner and motherhood. Choosing Steve would fast-forward her right through that chapter, which she's not ready for.

"So you're saying this is an age thing?" says Karyn.

"It's a *stage* thing. My husband is around eleven years older than I am, but when we met, we were both in the same stage: ready to get married and start a family. The age difference didn't matter. You and Steve, on the other hand, are in different stages, and your life circumstances make it really hard to meet in the middle."

"In other words, I want Steve in five years from now. After my career is established, when I'm ready to settle down. When his kids are older and maybe won't need him as much. But . . ."

"But . . . ?"

"I also wish it was now, because Steve is amazing."

"That's why ending this would be a big gamble. Logistics and timing aside, you two are a great match. It's not guaranteed that you'll find this kind of chemistry again. I agree that you can't commit to a situation you can't live with now, but you also can't expect that when you're ready in five years, your husband will automatically be there, waiting for you. You'll have to redo the work you've already done to find Steve."

Claire groans. "Why is this so hard?"

"Because you have to choose between two things you deeply care about."

After a minute, Karyn says, "I know what I'm really afraid of: admitting this isn't going to work."

"It's painful," I say. "You had a wonderful happenstance meeting straight out of a movie that just doesn't hold in reality. At the end of the day, you know this won't work. But, wow, how sad and hard it is to walk away."

"Right," she says, her voice breaking. "I don't want to end it, but I have to."

For clarity purposes, I ask, "Even if this could be your only shot with Steve?"

Karyn sighs. "I think if I stay with him now, I'd end up letting go of him later anyway. Better to save us both the extra heartache."

Good answer.

"Alright, Karyn. You know what to do."

## Rachel and Nick

Rachel has never wanted to live anywhere but Colorado. She was born here, went to college here, and has made a happy career for herself as a textile conservationist at the Denver Museum of Art. At twenty-nine, her days are filled with antiquated silks from China, flax cloth used to wrap the Neolithic dead, Egyptian linen found near the Dead Sea, the cotton aprons of Victorian scullery maids, and courtier gowns made from taffeta and crepe. And she gets paid for it.

Naturally, Rachel only dates men who live in the Denver area; dating outside Denver would only make things complicated when she has no intention of leaving. She tends to see the same candidates in her dating app feed, and at this point, she's either gone out with or rejected most of them. But then one night, to her surprise, she sees a new face online: Nick's. According to his profile, he's thirty with rugged good looks and knows how to spell, punctuate, and even write a joke. There's a cute dog in the picture with him.

Rachel swipes right.

Just a few minutes later, Nick sends her a message, which quickly turns into a chat, which turns into a text, which turns into a phone call, which turns into a date.

They meet at a cafe not far from the DMA, so Rachel can hop over after work. She's pleased to see that Nick is just as attractive as his picture and is gracious enough to pay for her Earl Grey and scone with cream.

"You sure you're not British?" Nick jokes.

She smiles. "I'm as Coloradan as you can get. What about you?"

"I was born in St. Louis, but I moved here with my parents about six years ago."

"What made you follow them to Denver?"

"I live with them. My dad got a job here, so I came, too."

"You live with your parents?" Rachel asks with surprise. She knows that, in many cultures, it's typical for more than one generation to live under the same roof until the child marries, and maybe even after. But she hasn't met many people in that situation before.

"I mean, not *with* them, with them," says Nick. "I live in an apartment on the bottom floor of their house. They get help with the mortgage and a tenant they can trust. I get affordable rent and I can see them every day. It's a win-win."

"That's nice that you get along so well. I'm close to my parents, but they can drive me crazy sometimes. I don't know if I could handle living in the same house, even if it was in my own apartment."

"Oh, don't worry. They drive me crazy, too," says Nick. "If my rent is late, I get an earful."

Rachel isn't sure how to respond to that, so she just says, "I bet."

"So tell me," says Nick. "How does a person become a textile conservationist?"

Usually, Rachel would opt for the short explanation from college to her current job, but for some reason, she finds herself telling him about her grandmother, Betty, who repaired costumes at the Metropolitan Museum of Art. When she retired, Betty moved in with Rachel and her parents, teaching Rachel about fabrics, design, and sewing. "I fell in love with it," Rachel says. "There's nothing else I've ever wanted to do."

"You're lucky to have a job you love that also connects you to a person you love," Nick replies.

She's never heard it put so succinctly, but he's absolutely right. She realizes now why she told him about her grandmother: Nick is a person who pays attention.

"What do you do?"

"I'm a manager at Petco. Nothing exciting. Just pays the bills."

"We all have to," says Rachel. She's never been one to judge people by their careers, nor has status and achievement ever been a factor in her choice of friends or partners. One of her best friends, for example, works at Trader Joe's for the pleasant environment and quality medical coverage. While she is more than capable of succeeding in a more demanding or lucrative job, this friend values her mental health and free time to read and make art. It's not about what people do for a living, in Rachel's book, but what they're living to do.

The rest of the date passes quickly and pleasantly; Rachel is surprised by how much she enjoys talking to Nick, with whom she discovers a shared love of punk music.

"Wait, *no one* knows Warsaw Pakt except me!" Rachel exclaims.

"Are you kidding?" Nick replies. "'Dog Fight' is one of my all-time favorite songs!"

Right there, in the middle of the cafe, the two of them start singing the chorus to the amusement of the other patrons, who applaud them when they're done. Nick stands up and bows. Rachel laughs.

After they leave the cafe, Rachel walks Nick to his car, a sleek Acura TLX, with a backseat filled with bags from different retail stores: Foot Locker, Dick's Sporting Goods, Uniqlo.

"Can I take you out to dinner this week?" Nick asks.

Rachel sees no reason to say no.

A few nights later, they go to a Brazilian steakhouse that's famed for its delicious food and extremely pricey menu. Rachel has no idea how he can afford dinner at a place like this, but asking him feels inappropriate. So she enjoys her meal and, at his urging, orders multiple drinks and an indulgent dessert. Nick is gracious, respectful, and engaging, asking her thoughtful questions and paying attention to her answers. He makes Rachel feel seen.

On their third date, Nick arrives with a present: a beautiful and hefty coffee-table book called *Costumes of the Metropolitan Museum of Art*. Rachel knows this book isn't cheap; she's eyed it herself a few times online but couldn't justify buying it. She's amazed that he got it for her.

"This is really generous," she says. "Are you sure . . . ?"

"When I saw it in a bookstore, it felt like a sign. I knew you needed to have it."

"Thank you. Can I ask you something?"

"Yeah, sure," says Nick.

"How can you . . . afford this stuff?"

Nick smiles. "I'm American. I live my life on credit."

Rachel is also American, but she was raised to live within her means. She earned scholarships and worked her way through college so she wouldn't graduate with mountains of debt. Sure, she might use a credit card sometimes for surprise expenses, but only if she knows she can pay it off quickly. The idea of living on credit is not one that sits well with her.

Still, she really likes Nick, so she continues to go out with him. They have a great time together, hiking at Red Rocks and seeing a concert in the amphitheater, going out for brunch and a movie matinee, and eating at some of the city's best restaurants—all courtesy of Nick. Rachel is uncomfortable with him spending so much on her (especially since she suspects it's well beyond his means) but he insists.

Then one night, just a few hours before their scheduled date, Nick calls apologetically to cancel. "I'm moving," he says. "I have to have everything cleaned out by Sunday."

"Wow, that's fast. Where are you moving?"

"Into my parent's house."

"I thought you had the apartment."

"They got a tenant for it. I was behind on rent, so . . ."

"How behind?"

"Four months."

"Oh." Rachel isn't sure if she's more disturbed by what he's saying or the fact that he sounds so chipper about it.

"It's great, though, because I don't have to pay any rent. And I'm saving on car payments because my parents took over the loan," says Nick.

"They're paying for your car?"

"They needed a second one anyway, so when the bank said they were going to repo, my parents decided to pay my balance and keep the car until I could pay them back."

In other words, Rachel realizes, Nick has hit a financial bottom and his parents are bailing him out.

"Did you ever think about changing your spending habits?" she asks gingerly. "Maybe then it would be easier to stay on top of bills."

"Yeah, I know, but I like nice things. And if I can afford them . . ."

"But that's the thing, Nick. You *can't* afford them."

"I will now that my expenses have gone down. I basically just put money in my pocket!"

That's when Rachel realizes she has a decision to make.

The next day she and I sign onto a Zoom chat, where she fills me in on the story with Nick. "It's one thing to live in your parents' house and work a low-level job if you have the end goal of saving for the next phase," she says. "I lived with my parents during grad school and worked nights so I could support myself when I graduated. I get it. But I don't think Nick has the same idea. He's happy to go on living with his parents so he can overspend with no big consequences. It's immature. A guy like him will go from draining his parents to draining his partner."

"I agree that what you're seeing could be a yellow or even a red flag," I say, "but before you make a decision, tell me, what is he bringing to this relationship?"

"He's a great guy. Insightful, smart, really respectful and generous. Good listener. I've never dated anyone who takes such an active interest in my life."

"Those are big plusses. It sounds like, if the spending issues are resolved, he could be a wonderful partner."

"That's why I keep going out with him. But I don't think the spending issues will be resolved, because he doesn't think it's a problem. Which is an even bigger problem."

Rachel has hit the nail on the head. Everyone has baggage, but a relationship can still be successful if you're self-aware and willing to grow. But if you don't see a problem in the first place, you've lost before the game has even begun.

"The bottom line is that Nick doesn't take responsibility for himself," says Rachel. "The spending and debt makes that clear. I want a partner to build a future with, not someone whose messes I have to clean up."

"Even with all the other wonderful things he has to offer?"

"It's already getting hard to see those things, and we're only a month in," she replies.

"Alright. So, Rachel, you're 100 percent sure you don't want to give it another shot?"

"Absolutely. Maybe the financial stuff is worth the tradeoff for someone else. But it isn't for me."

## CHAPTER TEN TIP

# Breaking Up: Serve a Compliment Sandwich

When it's time to end a relationship, you want to do it like a *mensch*. Even if this person is not your person, they have given you time and energy. That's why you should serve your breakup with a "Compliment Sandwich."

Here's your recipe:

### INGREDIENTS*

Respect

Gratitude

Appreciation

Kindness

Courtesy

1. Open the conversation with a compliment. Note something about them that you appreciate and highlight with anecdotes. (*"You're one of the most gracious people I've ever dated. When my friend forgot your name, you went out of your way to make sure she didn't feel bad. That's a wonderful quality."*)

2. Add on a clear and kind explanation for why it won't work. Be generous with "I" statements. (*"I admire your ambition and commitment to your career, but I'm looking for someone who is ready to settle down and focus on family."*)

3. Should they want to mix in questions, be sparing with your answers. (*"You're a very nice person, but our personalities aren't a match."*) If they did something wrong, tell them so respectfully. (NOTE: DO NOT ENGAGE IN AN ARGUMENT. IT WILL RUIN THE RECIPE.)

---

\* Ghosting is not an alternative to this recipe.

4. Close the sandwich with another compliment. (*"You are going to make a fantastic partner for the right person."*)

5. Wish them the best and end the conversation on a positive note.

Bon appétit!

CHAPTER ELEVEN

# Soulmate Clarity

Amanda is the kind of woman who knows exactly what she wants. As a kid watching Dominique Dawes compete in the Olympics, she knew instinctively that she was meant to become a gymnast, performing at the highest level, breaking records and winning medals. Raised by a single mom in North Philadelphia with little disposable income, Amanda babysat, raked leaves, and walked dogs to pay for gymnastics lessons—all while keeping her grades at an A average. She kept herself on a regimented schedule so that she could spend as much time as possible in the gym, and read everything she could get her hands on about anatomy, physiology, and physics. The results paid off: Amanda competed at the national level and showed promise of becoming a professional athlete. However, when she was sixteen, a car accident caused by a drunk driver broke Amanda's leg in six places. She spent two months in the hospital and had multiple surgeries. In the end, she recovered, but her days of gymnastics were over.

It was a low moment for Amanda. Her dreams had been shattered. For many weeks, she woke up, went to school, then came home and got into bed until the next day, when she repeated the cycle. She barely ate. Finally, Amanda's coach came to see her.

"I know how devastated you are," her coach said. "It's not easy to lose something you've worked so hard for. But just because you can't compete anymore doesn't mean you're not still a gymnast. You know more about the sport than anyone I know. I think you'd make an amazing coach."

That was all it took to get Amanda out of bed. She began working as an apprentice under her coach, teaching gymnastics at the same gym where she'd trained. She discovered that it was just as exciting to watch her students progress as it was when she did it herself. By the time she reached college, Amanda had a new dream: to help young women build their confidence and heal trauma through gymnastics.

Amanda took all the drive and focus that made her a star athlete and poured it into coaching, earning herself a growing number of devoted students. She also earned a dual degree in social work and business and bought the gym from her old coach. Today, all of her classes are booked solid. Her students adore her, especially the select few she coaches for serious competition.

And now, on this unseasonably warm New Year's Day, Amanda is celebrating a high note in her career. At the moment, she's surrounded by a hyped-up gaggle of middle-school girls who, like Amanda, are wearing lavish costumes, headdresses of feathers and flowers, and brightly colored makeup. They shriek and hug each other in triumph, having just spent the last two hours flipping and dancing up Broad Street in the world-famous Mummers Parade.

"You were amazing! I'm so beyond proud of you!" Amanda says. "Gymnastics begins with talent, but it's also about hard work and sacrifice. You all have given everything you've got, and look what you've accomplished." Her voice fills with emotion. "When I couldn't be a gymnast anymore, I thought I'd lost everything. But it gave me everything, because now I get to be your coach."

The tallest girl in the group slings an arm around her shoulders and squeezes. "Awwww, Amanda . . ."

Amanda wipes a tear away and squares her shoulders. "Alright, ladies. I think you deserve to celebrate!"

The girls clap and cheer, then head off with their families. One man from the group, however, stays behind.

"Hi, I'm Matt," he says. "Olivia's brother?"

"Oh, hi! Thanks for coming out," Amanda replies, doing her best to cover her surprise. Olivia, an eighth-grader, has mentioned an older brother, which Amanda assumed meant college age. But this man, dressed in a sweatshirt and jeans with a baseball cap, looks to be in his thirties. He is also, Amanda notices, very nice-looking.

"Wouldn't miss it," says Matt. "Olivia has been talking about this for months. Well, this, and you. She always says how amazing you are—and she's right. What you said to them today was inspiring."

Amanda blushes. "I just talk to them the way I would want someone to talk to me."

"Whatever you're doing, it's working. I've never seen my sister happier."

"I'm so glad to hear it. Thank you."

Matt clears his throat. "Could I take you out?"

"Oh!" Amanda says in surprise. She looks down at her wild costume, then back up at him. "Now?"

"That's up to you. I'm free if you are."

"I should probably change first . . ."

"Also up to you. I think you look great."

Amanda laughs. "Tell you what. I'll give you my number, then I'll go home to shower and change. We can meet up later if that works for you?"

"Yeah. Sounds great."

## Date One

Three hours later, they sit across the table from each other, munching on pad thai and talking like they've known each other for years. Amanda learns that Matt is thirty-three and an air traffic controller at Philadelphia International Airport. "I was always obsessed with flying," Matt explains, "but I have Ménière's disease. It's an inner-ear thing that causes vertigo and balance issues, so becoming a pilot was out. So I went into the control tower instead."

Matt's story resonates with Amanda, who recalls how her life changed after the car accident. She tells him the whole story and how it led her to becoming a coach. "I've put everything I have into these girls, and we have come so far. Being at the Mummers Parade felt like a huge win."

"Olivia felt that way, too," says Matt. "She said being in a parade was more exciting than her birthday."

"So cute. Is she your only sibling?"

"Yep. Twenty years between us. My parents tried to have other kids after I was born, but no go. Then my mom had a surprise pregnancy in her mid-forties."

"That's crazy!"

"Tell me about it. Imagine being in college and finding out your mom is having a baby!"

"How did you feel about it?"

"Excited. I always wanted a little brother or sister. And Olivia was the sweetest baby. I spent a lot of time with her, helping out and playing with her. And that's kind of how it's always been."

For Amanda, this reflects beautifully on Matt's character. Plenty of twenty-year-olds would resent giving up their status as an only child and distance themselves or even antagonize their new, younger sibling. But Matt was simply happy to have a sister and opened his heart to her with no hesitation.

"Well, I guess you and I have something in common," Amanda says. "We both think the world of Olivia."

"She and I also think you're pretty spectacular."

Amanda blushes again.

"I'd like to see you again," Matt says.

Amanda considers this for a second. Like her career as a gymnast, she has always had a very clear picture of the man she wants: tall, dark, and handsome; muscular build; intelligent; dashing; passionate; and confident. (Think Jason Momoa or Idris Elba.) Matt has some of these bases covered: he's tall and handsome, though his coloring is much lighter than her dream man's. He's in decent shape, but nowhere near the bulky type that Amanda imagines will make her feel safe and protected. Intelligence, check; he used the word "effusive" in a sentence and Amanda almost swooned. Matt is also kind, gentle, and easygoing, which is technically a plus, but she's always pictured someone with a stronger, more take-charge personality. The confidence factor is there, but in a much quieter, more earnest way than the charming Casanova she envisions. As for passion, Amanda guesses, only time will tell. And she wants to stick around to find out.

"Sure," she replies. "I think we can manage that."

## Date Two

On their next date, Matt takes Amanda to Only Vinyl, a record store on South Street with booths where you can sample the goods. Matt says he used to cut school to come here with his friends and listen to everything from Green Day to Etta James to Joan Jett to Fleetwood Mac. "Personally, I think I got a much better education here," he says.

Amanda flips through the titles until she comes upon a record that makes her smile: "What I Like About You" by the Romantics.

"A classic," Matt says approvingly.

"My mom and I used to dance to this song."

"So let's listen to it."

They slide into a booth together, and when the familiar chords begin, Amanda jumps out of her seat. "Sorry, but I can't not dance to this."

She rocks her shoulders and hips and shakes her head wildly, giving herself over to the music with abandon. She moves like someone completely comfortable and in tune with her body.

Matt laughs. "You do that a lot better than I do."

"Let's see what you've got," she says.

"No, really, I'm the worst dancer in recorded history."

"Prove it!"

Amanda pulls Matt to his feet and discovers that he's right. Matt's movements are stiff, jerky, and completely out of sync with the music. And his dance face makes him look like he's in pain. Amanda's so surprised, she stops dancing.

"I told you!" he says, laughing.

Amanda cracks up. "You're terrible!"

This makes them both laugh harder, until they're doubled over and out of breath.

"Look, you brought it on yourself," Matt says as they walk out of the record store. "I took you out to listen to music, not dance. That part was all you."

"I take full responsibility," Amanda replies with mock solemnity. "I guess ballroom dancing is out for our next date . . ."

"Hmm . . . is this you asking me out again?"

Amanda smiles. "Sounds like it."

And so it continues. Amanda takes Matt to a billiards bar, where she trounces him in every game. They make candles at Paddywax, laughing when Amanda's comes out looking like a lopsided carrot. Matt reserves dinner at a small bookstore restaurant and entertains Amanda by reading her Edgar Allan Poe aloud in a scary voice. At a double feature at the drive-in, an exhausted Amanda falls asleep on Matt's shoulder and he dozes off soon after. They wake up the next morning to an empty parking lot—then go out for breakfast.

Their first disagreement comes on a day trip to Amish Country, when they hit gridlock traffic on their way out of the city. Amanda had recommended that they leave early, but Matt, as usual, misplaced his keys and they lost half an hour while he looked for them. As they set off, Amanda recommended that Matt take back roads instead of the main highway, but after a long deliberation, he decided to stick with the driving directions on Waze. Now they're at a full stop on 76, with no sign of movement ahead. With each passing minute stuck in the car, Amanda feels herself becoming increasingly frustrated and anxious.

"Looks like a horse and buggy would get us there faster," Matt jokes.

Amanda doesn't laugh. "Or if we'd gone the back way, like I said."

"I didn't want to get lost."

"We have Waze, Matt. And I grew up going to Amish Country. I could get you there with my eyes closed." She hears how self-righteous she sounds, but can't stop herself from trying to grab control in an out-of-control situation.

Matt picks up on her energy and replies with an edge. "Then maybe *you* should have driven."

She rolls her eyes and looks out the window, mumbling something under her breath.

"What was that?" Matt says.

"I *said* it wouldn't have happened if you had gotten your act together."

"What is that supposed to mean?"

Amanda knows she should just leave it, but she's so tense she can't help but explode. "It *means* that you held us up by losing your keys, then going back and forth forever about which way to go, even though I clearly said what we should do. And now you can't even say you made a mistake!"

"Okay! I was wrong! Is that what you want? You were right and I was wrong." He sighs with exasperation, then says, "Though, honestly . . ."

"What?"

"Honestly, I don't mind being stuck here because I'm with you."

Amanda surprises them both by bursting into tears.

"What's wrong?" Matt says. "What did I say?"

"Nothing. You said exactly the right thing," she sniffles.

"Why are you crying, then?"

"Traffic scares me, okay? Since the car accident, I want to get where I need to go as quickly as possible. The longer you're on the road, the bigger the chance that something could happen."

"Oh," Matt says gently. "Why didn't you tell me?"

"Trauma isn't sexy."

He takes her hand. "You're sexy to me, Amanda. All of you. Not just the great parts."

Amanda is amazed. Not just by what he's said, but by his vulnerability and compassion in the midst of an argument. In seconds, he diffused the entire conflict and made her feel safe. This is a new experience for Amanda, who has known many people, herself included, who have sacrificed connection for the sake of being right. But, clearly, Matt values relationships more than winning.

Even more surprising is the effect that Matt's quiet, kind declaration had on her. It was nothing like the grand, passionate gestures Amanda has always longed for, like Adam Sandler serenading Drew Barrymore over an airplane loudspeaker, but somehow, it has completely swept her off her feet.

Matt turns off at the next exit as Waze reroutes, and grins at Amanda. "Alright, Captain. Lead us to Amish Country."

After that outing, Matt and Amanda's relationship deepens in a whole new way. Amanda realizes that she's considering Matt as a real contender, someone with whom there might be a future.

Apparently, the feelings are mutual. "Matty's totally obsessed with you," Olivia tells Amanda in class. "You're, like, all he talks about. Can you please marry him and be my sister?"

Amanda rolls her eyes playfully. "Get on the balance beam, goofball."

That evening, she gets a text from Matt. *Heard my sister proposed. Congratulations. Maybe you want to meet her parents?*

The invitation makes Amanda smile. If a future with Matt is in the works, this would certainly be a step in that direction. But she's also hesitant to say yes. He isn't exactly who she pictured for herself. He has a lot of great qualities, but is he really the one? What if she connects with the family and it doesn't work out?

Before replying, she decides that a conversation with me is in order. Over a lunch of falafel and tahini milkshakes at Goldie in downtown Philly, she gives me a rundown of her relationship with Matt.

"I'm waiting for the problematic part," I say. "So far, all I've heard is what a great match you two are."

"True, but . . . he isn't what I pictured for myself."

"What did you picture?"

She gives me a detailed description of her dream man— basically a hunky mix of superhero, Bridgerton brother, and Rhodes Scholar.

"So what you're saying is, Matt isn't your unicorn."

Everyone has a vision of their perfect mate, someone with the exact looks and personality you find most attractive and possessing the same values and dreams that you have. Naturally, your relationship with this person will be passionate, exciting, and right in every way. All you have to do is find them.

Bad news: you never will.

While this amalgam of perfection is a lovely idea, the person you imagine is a unicorn: a mythical creature that exists only in your imagination.

Sorry.

The good news is that there are a multitude of flesh-and-blood humans who are potentially great partners. They might even be a dead ringer for your unicorn, but come with a package of flaws that you will have to accept in exchange for the whole package. After all, isn't it better to find an imperfect person who does exist than hold out for a unicorn that doesn't? Or worse, discard a wonderful, living and breathing partner because they don't measure up to the unicorn in your head? I've seen too many people squander beautiful relationships for this reason, and frankly, it's not a smart move.

"Just because Matt isn't what you envisioned for yourself doesn't mean he's not the right match for you," I say. "In fact, I know a lot of people who find a partner that's nothing like their unicorn, and they're happier than they ever imagined."

Matthew Perry summed this sentiment up perfectly in the movie *Fools Rush In*, when he professes his love to Salma Hayek: "You're everything I never knew I always wanted."

"It's time to flip reality and fantasy," I explain. "Break up with your unicorn and embrace what the person in front of you has to offer."

Amanda's not sold. "But why should I settle for less than I want?"

"Not less, just different."

"Isn't that the same thing?"

"Not at all. Amanda, you know better than anyone about adjusting dreams to reality. You gave everything to become a gymnast, but a car accident forced you to let that dream go. Instead of being bitter about it, you found a new dream. And look how happy it's made you. You're still getting what you wanted, just in a different way than you thought."

Amanda's eyes brighten with recognition. "I got it. But I have a question."

"Shoot."

"If I'm not measuring against my usual criteria, how do I know if Matt *is* right for me?"

Ladies and gentlemen, welcome to Soulmate Clarity.

Soulmate Clarity is a diagnostic tool for relationships that I developed after speaking to hundreds of clients trying to untangle their own thoughts and feelings. Over and over, I would hear, "I think he's great, but I don't know . . ." or "I feel like it could work with her, but I'm not sure . . ." They were eyeing the bridge to real commitment, debating whether or not they should cross it. Using my own knowledge of relationships, compatibility, and human psychology, I presented their thoughts back to them and offered my advice on next steps. Then came the inevitable question: "Yeah, but how do you know?"

I realized that in the modern age of information, people need hard data—even if it's about something conventionally abstract, like thought and emotion. By seeing it in front of them in black and white, something concretizes in the brain. They suddenly have *facts* they can use to make a confident decision, versus just taking my word for it. This is especially helpful to me, because I'm not here to convince anyone to do anything. My job is to simply hold up a mirror so you can see things as they (and you!) really are.

Without going into too much technical detail, Soulmate Clarity combines your thoughts and feelings with my expertise to measure compatibility and relationship longevity. We divide qualities, fears, and bothers, concepts we discussed in previous chapters, into three categories—aligned (green), acceptable (yellow), and potential deal-breaker (orange)—and quantify them based on importance to you and whether or not you feel your partner meets the criteria. These results, which are presented in percentages and illustrated with color-coded pie charts, clearly show you where things are working, where some support might be needed, and where things are likely to go bust. To greenlight a relationship, we are looking for 70 percent alignment or more.

The beauty of Soulmate Clarity is that it's completely objective. It's your brain and heart on paper, computed into hard data that I simply report back. This is a gift, whether the chart is a good or bad one (and I've seen plenty of both). When the ratios are 70 percent+ with lots of green alignment, you get my blessing and the confidence to move forward with something great. When the pie charts show a majority of orange potential deal-breakers, you've got incontrovertible evidence that the relationship is the *Titanic*, post-iceberg. Even when clients insist, "But I love them!", all I have to do is point them back to the data: "Maybe so, but according to you, this will never, ever work out."

In most healthy relationships, the pie charts show a mix of green alignment and yellow acceptables with a smaller percentage of orange potential deal-breakers. "There's no such thing as an 'all-green' relationship," I explain to Amanda, "just like there's no such thing as a unicorn. At the end of the day, two imperfect people who have lots in common decide they are willing to accept the other person's flaws with the whole package. It may not be as glamorous as the love story and hero of your fantasies, but it's the best that real life has to offer. So let's see how you and Matt measure up."

First we talk about nonphysical qualities that are important to Amanda—not necessarily qualities that Matt has, but ones that she deeply values. While a partner might not have every one of your desired attributes, if they have the majority (say, seven or eight out of ten) to the degree you're looking for, you're on the right track.

In typical Amanda fashion, she quickly lists ten qualities she wants: family-oriented, consistent, trustworthy, responsible, funny, intelligent, patient, respectful, kind, and passionate. First, we rate how important each one is to her. Then we see which of these qualities apply to Matt, and how much.

"Matt has most of these qualities," Amanda says. "He's a good, steady guy; super smart; always shows up; he's kind to me; and he's connected to his family. But it's funny. I wouldn't consider him a passionate person—at least, not outwardly so—but now that I'm dating him, it doesn't seem as important as I thought."

So we strike it from the list and replace it with "openhearted."

"Would you say that's Matt?" I ask.

Amanda thinks back to his story about baby Olivia and smiles. "Yeah, I'd say so."

Next, we talk about Amanda's relationship-centered fears. We've discussed fears in previous chapters, so I don't have to remind you that we all have them. Compatibility is about how much your partner *triggers* these fears, which Soulmate Clarity will tell you. Amanda knows her fears right off the bat: divorce, being a single parent, not being heard, and losing her financial independence.

"How much does Matt trigger these fears?"

"In terms of the divorce or single-mom thing, barely at all. His parents have been happily married forever and he's only ever been in monogamous relationships. He's also been with the same job for nine years and is supportive of my work, so financially, it seems fine."

"What about not being heard?"

Matt's response to Amanda's anxiety meltdown flashes in her mind. "Well, he doesn't always automatically get it, but when I explain how I feel to him, he's responsive and kind."

"I think it's safe to say that most people don't 'get it automatically' because we're not mind readers," I reply. "But it seems like you are able to communicate in an effective and constructive way, and he puts in the effort to understand you."

"I think you're right. But I still have this irrational fear about the relationship falling apart. With my parents' history, I'm worried that the little things that may not bother me now will grow and grow until the relationship combusts."

"So let's talk about those bothers and see how likely it is that what you're afraid of will happen. What about Matt bothers you?"

As we know, being bothered by things is human. A good partner is someone who sets off those bothers to the minimum degree. Or, they're so fabulous in most other respects that you're willing to learn to live with their bothersome parts.

"He's messy and disorganized; the man is constantly losing his keys. He's self-conscious and also a big overthinker. It takes him *forever* to make a decision. He can also be a bit of a people-pleaser, you know, the kind of guy who apologizes when you bump into him?"

I chuckle. "Okay. How much do these things bother you?"

According to Amanda, people-pleasing and self-consciousness aren't as bothersome as disorganization and overthinking, which she says is an eight on a scale of one to ten. "My years of training have made me a really regimented person. I have a tight schedule and a system for everything. Disorganization and chaos make me nuts. I also don't have the patience to think things to death; I make my decisions and don't look back. Sometimes, I have to wait twenty minutes for Matt to get his stuff together and then another twenty minutes to decide where we're going. By the time we leave I want to lose it. Imagine if we had kids in the mix!"

"So you'd consider this a potential deal-breaker?" I ask.

"No, no, no. It's annoying, but I wouldn't end the relationship over it." Amanda hears what she's just said and stops for a second.

"Wait a minute. This is usually a giant trigger for me. I've broken up with guys for less. But in the scheme of my relationship with Matt, this doesn't feel like a potential deal-breaker at all."

I smile at her. "Very interesting."

With that, I enter the rest of Amanda's data, run the script, and the results come up within seconds. The "qualities" pie chart is 80 percent green, 10 percent yellow. "Fears" shows 60 percent green and 40 percent yellow. Happily, neither one contains a trace of orange. Only in "Bothers" do we find that yellow and green are evenly divided at 40 percent each, with a 20 percent orange slice.

"*Mazel tov!*" I say. "According to the data, you and Matt are well over 70 percent aligned. You have a great foundation to build a strong and happy relationship."

Amanda grins. "Pretty good."

"Worth giving up a unicorn for?"

She laughs. "I'd say so."

I point out the slice of orange on her "Bothers" chart, which indicates how much his disorganization and overthinking trigger her. "I want you to be realistic about this. Do not assume that, if you continue with the relationship, Matt will change. Expect that if you choose him, you are choosing to take on these issues. That means developing your own tools to handle them over time. He may never get better in this regard, but you will get better at managing it."

"In other words, I might have to stop being such a control freak?" Amanda says with a laugh.

"That's one way of putting it."

Amanda looks at the chart again and shakes her head in disbelief. "This is crazy. I knew things were good between us, but I didn't realize they were *this* good."

"Sometimes, you have to see it in front of you before it all makes sense."

Later that night, Amanda returns Matt's text: *Tell Olivia's parents that I'm free tomorrow night.*

## CHAPTER ELEVEN TIP

## Clarity Questionnaire

1. Do our values appear to be aligned based on the information that I have today? Write 3–5 concrete examples.

   *Example: He is devoted to his family and my value is having a close-knit family.*

2. Do I enjoy their personality? Make a list of 3–5 things that I enjoy most.

   *Example: She is extroverted but not loud, which is important to me because I'm sensitive to noise.*

3. Knowing that we all have fears, does this person trigger mine to a sustainable degree?

   *Example: I have a fear of abandonment, but he is consistent with checking in and communication. He is also there for me without me having to ask.*

4. Knowing that we all have bothers, does this person trigger mine to a manageable degree?

   *Example: She is consistently late, but I appreciate that she gives me a heads-up so I can manage my schedule.*

5. If this person was not my physical ideal, have this person's looks grown on me?

   *Example: In the beginning, I wasn't repulsed, but he was better than neutral. Over ten dates, I feel more comfortable with him and he seems to be easy on the eyes now.*

# Conclusion

The journey we have embarked upon through the pages of this book reflects a deep dive into the heart of what it means to love and be loved—with authenticity, empathy, and unwavering honesty. As we peel back the layers of successful relationships, we discover that at their core, they are crafted not from perfection, but from the willingness to show up, be seen, and love fiercely despite the uncertainties of life and the path ahead.

As you move forward, don't lose sight of the power of a kind word, a genuine smile, or the strength found in a shared silence. These moments build bridges between hearts, fostering a love that is resilient, nurturing, and deeply fulfilling.

A good match is about finding someone whose values align with ours, whose spirit complements our own, and with whom we can share the profound beauty of being understood.

It's as much about discovering ourselves as it is about discovering another. It's a journey that asks us to be brave, to stay open, and to embrace the beauty of our own becoming. With every step, with every leap of faith, we move closer to the partnership we seek—and the partnership we are destined to find.

Let's carry forward the wisdom that "love," in its truest form, is a verb—an action that demands our engagement, patience, and courage. It's about allowing ourselves the vulnerability to trust, to hope, and to believe in the possibility of a love that's actually so much richer and deeper than the "happily ever afters" of our favorite fairy tales.

So let this not be an end, but a beginning. A beginning of a new chapter in your life, where love is not just a possibility, but a reality waiting to unfold. Thank you for allowing me to guide you through this journey. May your path be filled with love, understanding, and joy.

*Aleeza*

# Appendix: The Five-Date Challenge

If you find dating complicated and confusing, you're not alone. It's not easy to get to know a prospective partner while making sense of your own thoughts, feelings, and expectations. It can be so overwhelming, many people are tempted to give up dating altogether.

But before you call it quits, let me offer a suggestion: the Five-Date Challenge.

This system, which I devised based on work with thousands of singles, offers a new approach to dating that will help you decide if your date has long-term potential. With just five simple practices, you can avoid the confusion and anxiety that lead daters to drag out a dead-end relationship or ditch a promising prospect too early. Instead, you can just relax and enjoy the ride.

Here's how the Five-Date Challenge works:

## 1. Commit to five dates, no more than five hours per date, and no more than five days between dates.

This timeline is foolproof for dating clarity. First, you commit to five dates before pulling the plug. This frees you from the post-date debate: yes or no? You can simply get to know the other person and collect information to consider later. During this five-date period, dates should last no longer than five hours; better to leave them wanting more than to overstay your welcome. Waiting no longer than five days between dates will keep the momentum going and get you to your decision faster.

By the end of five dates, you might be 100 percent sure this person isn't for you, and you can say goodbye with no regrets. On the other hand, you might discover something you didn't see at first and decide it's worth exploring more. Either way, you'll have given yourself the time to make a clear, conscious decision.

## 2. Don't talk to more than five people about dating.

When there are too many cooks in the kitchen, dinner will be a disaster. The same goes when you talk to too many people about your dating life; the symphony of voices will drown out your own. I recommend having a minimum of one person and no more than five to advise you, whether it be a spiritual figure, a parent, a mentor, or a married friend (singles may have no more clarity than you do!). Make sure your confidant has no agenda except to help you decide what's right for you.

## 3. Keep physical touch out of the equation (for at least the first five dates!).

Imagine that you've committed not to touch someone for five dates. After three dates, you decide you like them. After five dates, you *really* like them. You decide to extend the no-touching commitment to ten, then fifteen dates. By now, you *really, really* like them. If you haven't had any physical contact it's obvious that what you like is the person, not the pleasure of touching them.

This is why I recommend no touching while dating—or, at least, for the first five dates.

Most people look at me sideways when I make this suggestion, but I stand by it. Once physical touch is introduced into a relationship, it can't be undone. Our bodies and minds are designed to respond to it, and will convince us there's a connection where there might not be one (yet). Refraining from all physical contact for at least the first five dates is a surefire way to maintain your clarity as you get to know the other person. Some people even wait until they're married to touch for the first time, because they want to be 100 percent sure that they're choosing the other person with both eyes open.

"Love is blind," as they say, and I'll add that physical touch is blinding. Getting physical often leads people to ignore red flags, or even basic incompatibility, because their bodies are already off and running. It becomes all the more difficult to separate what you value on their inside from how they make you feel on the outside. Your time is precious; don't waste it with the wrong person because you confused physical chemistry for a real relationship.

On the other hand, intimacy and chemistry develop at hyperspeed when there's no physical touch. Without distractions, you can get to know each other more deeply and let the emotions percolate. Giving yourselves time to build anticipation makes it all the sweeter when you can finally touch each other. (Trust me on this one: holding my husband's hand for the first time under the wedding canopy was one of the most exciting moments of my life!)

**4. Find five strengths and five weaknesses in the person you're dating.**

You know a person well when you can identify the good and the not-so-good about them. Seeing only the good is infatuation, only the bad is a self-fulfilling prophecy. Over the course of your five dates, write down five things you like and five things you dislike about the other person. This will eventually help you decide if there's real potential for a relationship.

**5. Go on five different types of dates.**

Ever run into a teacher or coworker in the grocery store and felt . . . different around them? It's because different sides of people come out in different contexts. Doing a variety of activities or going to different places on dates will give you a fuller picture of the person you're trying to get to know. Whether it's their reaction to winning (or losing) a game, exploring a place neither of you have been before, or overcoming a challenge together, you'll be able to gather important information about who this person is and who you are when you're with them. Down the road, it will help you imagine a future with them—or not.

I never give advice I can't back up. After seeing hundreds of people reboot their dating lives through the Five-Date Challenge, I can say with full confidence: take the challenge and see the change!

May it give you clarity and confidence and bring you closer to finding your person.

# Resources

**Books**

*Get Real, Get Married* by Aleeza Ben Shalom

*The Five Love Languages: The Secret to Love That Lasts* by
   Gary Chapman

*Eight Dates: Essential Conversations for a Lifetime of Love* by John
   Gottman, PhD

*Marry Him: The Case for Settling for Mr. Good Enough* by
   Lori Gottlieb

*Nonviolent Communication: A Language of Life* by Marshall B.
   Rosenberg, PhD

*Feel the Fear . . . and Do It Anyway* by Susan Jeffers

*Slowing Down to the Speed of Life* by Richard Carlson


**Podcasts**

*Matchmaker, Matchmaker* with Aleeza Ben Shalom

*Where Should We Begin?* with Esther Perel

*Unlocking Us* with Brené Brown


**Other**

National Domestic Violence Hotline: 1-800-779-7233 or text *Start*
   to 88788

**Resources**

Love is Respect—National Teen Dating Abuse Hotline:
1-866-331-9474 or text 22522

Rape, Abuse, and Incest National Network (RAINN)—National
Sexual Assault Hotline: 1-800-656-4673

Department of Defense (DOD) Safe Helpline for Sexual
Assault: 1-877-995-5247

# Acknowledgments

This book was my baby. The idea for it grew in me for a long time, but it took quite a few people to help me form it into something tangible and deliver it into the world. First and foremost, thank you to my family. My husband, Gershon, keeps our home running while I travel the world, helping other people find partners with whom to build their homes. It's because of his complete belief in me that I can do what I do. Thank you, Gershon, for being my life partner and #1 fan. I'm always learning from our children, Dovid, Miriam, Moshe, Yehuda, and Avraham, who support and encourage me wholeheartedly, and who are willing to share their mom with the world. I'm so proud of the amazing people you are growing into every day. Thanks for taking this ride with me.

Rea Bochner, my writing buddy, teased out every drop of knowledge I had in my brain and helped me put it all into words. Thank you for the hours of work you put into this book alongside me, and for making me laugh along the way. I love a great match, and having you as my work wife is a match made in heaven.

The rest of my team (you know who you are) are all incredible people whose wisdom and dedication have taught me so much, professionally and personally. Thank you for always bringing your A-game, your ideas, and your passion, and for keeping an eye on the details. It's not hyperbole to say I could not be where I am without you.

Cece Lyra, my tireless agent, worked her tail off to help this book become a reality. She is a very talented matchmaker, finding just the right home for my vision. Thank you, Cece, for helping me make this book the best it could be and connecting me with publishers who believe in it just as much as I do.

The team at Union Square & Co. has been wonderful from the get-go. Thank you for being so passionate about this book, for helping me fine-tune it into something truly stellar, and for getting it into the hands of readers around the world.

I would have had nothing to write about if not for the thousands of past clients and couples I've worked with, as well as all the followers and fans who have hopped on the Aleeza train over the years. You all have taught me everything I know. Thank you for sharing your hearts, your heartbreaks, and your happy endings with me.

Last but far from least, thank you to the Creator, Hashem. You are the source of every breath, every blessing, every moment I've experienced in this incredible life. Thank you for the endless gifts you give me every day, and for the opportunity to leave Your world a little better than I found it.

# About the Author

**Aleeza Ben Shalom** is a renowned relationship coach and matchmaker who shot to international fame as the star of Netflix's *Jewish Matchmaking*. She is also the host of the *Matchmaker, Matchmaker* podcast. To date, she has successfully helped over 200 people make their way down the aisle, and has trained over 350 matchmakers and coaches. Originally from Philadelphia, Aleeza lives in Israel with her husband, five children, and two Aussiedoodles. To learn more about Aleeza and her dating and matchmaking courses, visit aleezabenshalom.com.